# PARTY OF ONE

## LIVING SINGLE WITH FAITH, PURPOSE & PASSION

Beth M. Knobbe

ST. ANTHONY MESSENGER PRESS
Cincinnati, Ohio

*For the gifts and the call of God are irrevocable.*
—Romans 11:29



Cover design by Connie Gabbert
Cover image ©Amanda Wingers
Book design by Mark Sullivan

LIBRARY OF CONGRESS CATALOGING-IN-PUBLICATION DATA
Knobbe, Beth M.
Party of one : living single with faith, purpose, and passion / Beth M. Knobbe.
p. cm.
Includes bibliographical references.
ISBN 978-0-86716-990-4 (alk. paper)
1. Single people—Religious life. I. Title. II. Title: Living single with faith, purpose, and passion.
BV4596.S5K56 2011
248.8'4—dc22
2011015022

ISBN 978-0-86716-990-4


Published by St. Anthony Messenger Press
28 W. Liberty St.
Cincinnati, OH 45202
www.AmericanCatholic.org
www.SAMPBooks.org

Printed in the United States of America.
Printed on acid-free paper.
11 12 13 14 15 5 4 3 2 1

## CONTENTS

## ACKNOWLEDGMENTS

I could not have written this book without the insights of many people who shared their stories with me. I especially want to thank our contributing authors whose essays put the joys and challenges of the single life into perspective with humor and grace.

To Lisa Biedenbach and everyone at St. Anthony Messenger Press, thank you for your collaboration and for believing in this project from the moment it first breathed life. Thanks also to BustedHalo.com for publishing "The Single Life: How I Stopped Dating and Started Living," written while much of this book was still being formed in my heart.

I owe special thanks to good friends on my journey through the single years, especially Abby Nall, Jenene Francis, JoEllen Cattapan, and Meredith McCarthy, who have prayed with me and for me throughout this project. Thank you for ensuring that my life is filled with adventure, excitement, and love, and for making sure that I always have a good story to tell.

My family constantly tells me how proud they are and how much they love me: Thanks to my parents Don and Dee Knobbe, a wonderful example of love and marriage for over forty years; my siblings and their spouses (Becky and Jim, Curtis and Iva, Anna and Chet, and Joe); my nieces and nephews who smother me with affection, provide me with endless laughter, and give me the great joy of being doting Aunt B. I am so blessed. I love you all.

Finally, I am grateful to the faith communities that have supported me and encouraged this call to live an intentional single life, especially the many friends from Old St. Patrick Church in Chicago and the students, staff, and associates of the Sheil Catholic Center at Northwestern University.

# PREFACE

Have you ever wondered "Is there something wrong with me?" because you're not in a relationship? Do you feel forever stuck at the kids' table at family gatherings? Do friends keep encouraging you to "put yourself out there" because the more you date, the more you increase your chances of finding the man or woman of your dreams? Has anyone ever suggested to you that being single is a selfish way to live? Do you find yourself putting your dreams on hold while you wait for marriage? Have you ever felt out of place at church because your faith community places so much emphasis on the importance of marriage and children?

If you answered "yes" to any of these questions, know that I wrote this book for *you.* In these pages I talk about the myths and the realities of being single and address the fears we singles face, the assumptions people make about us, and the questions we ask ourselves—especially when it becomes clear that the single life is becoming a permanent state in life and not just a passing phase on the way to something else.

My intent is to encourage Christians to approach singlehood with purpose and passion. I want you to *enjoy* being single, which is not always easy to do.

## What You Will Find Here

So often we singles are not taken seriously. Despite having very fulfilling and successful lives, singles are sometimes viewed as unfinished, flawed, naïve, or selfish. Furthermore, being single in today's world can be, at times, downright painful, lonely, and frustrating.

When we embrace the single life, we discover a deep sense of freedom, fulfilling relationships, unique opportunities for work and service, and ample space for God. We each have places where we find joy, issues with which we struggle, strategies for navigating the dating scene (if we decide to date at all), and ready responses to the questions we receive from family and friends.

In *Party of One: Living Single With Faith, Purpose & Passion,* I employ the insights of Scripture, spiritual sages, and ordinary people who show us that the single life can be a place of abundance and joy if we choose to welcome it. In each chapter I explore a different aspect of the single life and provide a reflection on a spiritual principle to guide you, as well as practical and spiritual advice for finding happiness and contentment during the single years.

To capture a fuller experience of the single-life experience, I invited friends, colleagues, and other singles to submit reflections for this book. These reflections shaped much of the book's content and provided crucial insights for how the spiritual life contributes to a satisfying single life. Contributors include those who are content to be single, those who are searching for someone, some who are dating, others who are in a serious relationship, and even a few who are no longer single but have made a permanent commitment to marriage or religious life.

You also will find suggestions for reading Scripture and questions for reflection suitable for individual or group use. Each of the book's four sections ends with "Try This"—my recommendations for how to integrate what you've just read into your own spiritual journey.

**What "Single" Means**

I wrote this book primarily for those who have never been married, those on their way to marriage, people who are in a relationship or wish to be in a relationship, singles content to not be dating anyone at the moment, and those who find themselves intentionally single with no strong desire toward marriage or religious life but who are willing to live with a sense of purpose, ready to respond to God's call in whatever way that unfolds.

I recognize that many people are single by circumstance and not always by choice, including those who are divorced, separated, and widowed. Many, for a variety of reasons, find themselves parenting alone or sharing parental duties with their child's father or mother outside of the context of marriage. Although I don't address these topics specifically, I hope you, too, will find words of encouragement and insight here.

Throughout my work on this project, I encountered people who exclaimed, "I have nothing positive to say about being single! Your readers surely won't want to hear from me." I also received inquiries from two friends, both of whom had recently broken off a significant relationship, asking, "When is the book going to be finished? I might need to read it soon!"

We can be angry, live with worry, bottle up our sadness, and continue to hope that the right person may be waiting around the corner. Or we can embrace the single life with gratitude, purpose, freedom, commitment, friendship, intimacy, and love—and yes, even find that living single can be a celebration—a *Party of One!*

How will you choose to live your one single life?

# INTRODUCTION

## How I Stopped Dating and Started Living[1]

Shortly before my thirtieth birthday, I decided I was tired of waiting for the right guy to come along and made what some people think is a radical choice. Instead of jumping onto the speed-dating circuit and signing up for an online dating service, I chose to stop dating. For the first time, I realized that being single is more than just waiting to get married.

I didn't see this decision as "giving up dating" as much as I was giving myself over to the things I'm most passionate about in life. I was committing to live my single life with a sense of purpose and intention, able to give myself wholeheartedly to my friendships, family, and volunteer activities. I was suddenly free from the anxiety heaped upon me by the expectation that I should be married.

Contrary to some misperceptions, I did not give up dating because of a bad experience or out of anger with a particular guy. My decision was precipitated by some much larger questions looming in my life: What does true love really look like? Who am I in love with, and is anyone in love with me? Is it truly God's desire for me to be married? What if God *wants* me to be single?

### Finding My True Vocation

All of these questions boiled down to a desire to find my true vocation. While growing up, I heard a lot about vocations, always presented as a call to the married life, religious life, or single life. The single life, however, was never given much credence, and the idea of choosing to be single was usually presented as a last resort.

Discovering one's vocation is more than deciding whether to get married, join the seminary, or enter a religious community. Finding your vocation in life answers the questions, "Who do you want to be with?" and "How do you want to be with them?"

I want to be with people in such a way that I can share my passion for God and live a life of service to others. This is something I've known for a very long time. It is my true calling in life; it is who I am. The more I reflected on this, the more I realized that the best way to live out this call is as a committed single person.

My choice to be single for the moment is not a choice to avoid relationships. In some ways, I'm actually choosing to be in deeper relationships with others. As single people, we often look for love and affection from people of the opposite sex. When I stopped looking for dating relationships, I developed closer relationships with my girlfriends, and I was free to enter into greater friendships with my guy friends. I had a wonderful and ever deepening relationship with God through prayer and found greater fulfillment through involvement with my church. I also had a supportive family (parents, siblings, cousins, nieces, and nephews) who provided love, affection, and affirmation for my dreams.

Not everyone is called to a life of intentional singleness. I suspect many who find themselves single wish their circumstances were different. Singles sometimes struggle with loneliness, anxiety, fear, pressure from family, and our own self-worth. Likewise, we are inclined to believe that the grass is greener on the other side of the relationship fence. Singles believe that married people have it all together, and married couples miss the carefree spirit of their single years. Marriage isn't easy; single life isn't easy either.

It is hard not to compare, especially when marriage is the norm in our society. And by speaking so strongly in favor of the single life, I certainly do not want to leave the impression that I am anti-marriage. I have watched my married friends exert a tremendous amount of love, heartache, and sacrifice to make their marriages work. I also feel blessed to count many men and women religious among my teachers, mentors, and colleagues in ministry. I know each of them has experienced a deep sense of fulfillment in their vocation and yet each of them has struggled from time to time with questions of commitment. Singles sometimes struggle with loneliness and fear, but they also experience deep satisfaction and joy. Marriage is not a permanent fix for one's personal flaws, discernment doesn't end once someone has taken vows, and being single doesn't have to mean being alone or without love.

**Being Single Feels "Right"**

Whether we are single for a brief time or forever, singleness is an invitation to discover who we are, to live our lives in the present, to not be trapped by our past or so consumed with the future that we fail to recognize the many gifts and opportunities that await us right now.

For some people being single feels "right" in the same way that meeting the man or woman of your dreams makes marriage the "perfect match" and others feel most "at home" by entering religious life, priesthood, or an intentional community. Whether by choice or by circumstance, single people find themselves freed up for something else. This freedom may be directed toward friendship, service, hospitality, or other pursuits.

My siblings who are married always said that you will "just know" when it's right. I have to say that this idea of being intentionally single feels much different than being on the dating scene, but for now, I just know, it feels right.

SECTION ONE

# Living Single With **Faith**

*Purpose*
*Humility*
*Wisdom*
*Gratitude*
*Forgiveness*
*Discernment*

CHAPTER ONE

# Living Single With **Purpose**

*The trajectory I imagined at sixteen was not the reality that I was living at age twenty-six. I hit twenty-six years old, and realized that the narrative of my life wasn't following the path I had imagined. I had to stop and ask myself, "Where is God taking me? And am I willing to go along with it?"*—Julia, 35

## Combating Single Myth #1: **Life Begins at Marriage**

For many years, I had a note taped to my bathroom mirror that said, "Life is a journey, not a destination." It reminded me that life is an adventure filled with excitement, growth, celebration, heartache, disappointment, and ordinary days. "I wished to live deliberately...," as Henry David Thoreau says, "...and not, when I came to die, discover that I had not lived."[1]

Many of us grew up with the image of a happily-ever-after ending. What little girl hasn't dreamed of walking down the aisle on her father's arm, dressed in a beautiful white gown, with the man of her dreams waiting at the front of the church? I'm sure many singles, at some point during adolescence or early adulthood, devised a plan or held an image of the ideal age to marry, when to have children and how many, where to live, and the kind of person we wanted to grow old with.

The old adage rings true: When we make plans, God laughs. Time passes, the mile markers that indicate a successful completion of our singlehood never appear and leave us wondering when our turn will come. Our hopes and dreams remind us of what is most important in life. They shape our values, determine the kinds of careers we pursue, and influence the friendships we maintain. Our lives unfold day by day and one decision at a time. When our personal histories are told, the end result is typically not the same as the lives we imagined for ourselves years earlier.

If you have ever found yourself saying, "When I get married, I will finally...," how do you fill in the blank? Do you say, "When I get married I will finally buy the house of my dreams, take a cruise, confront the issues of my past, or be at peace with myself?" But what happens in the meantime? What happens if we're left waiting five, ten, fifteen years or more for that special someone to walk through the door? Do you find yourself putting all your wishes on hold?

Many singles live with the myth that we need to wait until we are in a relationship before we can live the kind of life we want and do the things we love. Life does not start the moment you walk down the aisle. Life is happening in front of your very eyes! Life is not a dress rehearsal for when you have a relationship. So, what are you waiting for?

**Gratitude for the Intentional Journey:::** *Abby Nall*

Over coffee, I voiced doubts to my best friend about contributing to the theme of living the single life with intention. "I'm thirty-three years old," I said, "and am just starting over in a new career. My life hasn't taken an intentional path."

"Abigail," my girlfriend of seventeen years scolded, "you have been living intentionally more than anyone I know." She rattled off a list of activities I had pursued, opportunities I had taken, and accomplishments I had achieved. After silently thanking God for my friend's gift of perspective, I realized that I had associated "intention" with having a plan—a road map for navigating through life to some unknown (but somehow vitally important) destination.

As I reflected on our conversation, I began to consider "intention" as a compass providing direction for the course I was on in the *present moment*. With that in mind, the seemingly convoluted path of the past ten years of my adult life was transformed into a much more meaningful journey.

My "intentional compass" was what allowed me to accept that same friend's invitation when I was twenty-three, a college graduate waiting tables and trying to decide whether to pursue graduate studies. "Ab," she said, "I need a roommate, and you need to get the heck out of there." A month later the compass steered me into Chicago with no more than a résumé and the name of a temp agency. Ten years later, I am still grateful for being willing to make a change and open my life to new opportunities and experiences.

My "spiritual compass" led me to attend alone a new-parishioner welcome reception at the parish near my apartment. The only one who showed up that day, I was immediately recruited to serve at the Sunday evening Mass sponsored by the young adult group. Over the next few years, I was guided to become more involved in the group, eventually leading it, and this allowed me to meet wonderful people and become involved in a variety of activities.

My "personal growth compass" pointed me to taking guitar classes, creative writing workshops, martial arts instruction, and French lessons, as well as training for and running two marathons, joining a softball team, and even skydiving!

My "friendship compass" helped me cultivate strong relationships with girlfriends who have been an amazing source of laughter and support. It directed me to group adventures in Spain and Portugal, Hawaii, and Puerto Rico, cross-country road trips to help friends move to Seattle and Los Angeles, and to organizing a regular girls' night out.

My "career compass" navigated me toward two challenging and interesting jobs, but when I found myself hitting a wall regarding the next step, it opened my mind to the idea of career coaching. At twenty-nine, I was led to return to school full time to pursue a career in health-care, a decision that brings me daily joy and fulfillment.

Stepping back and reflecting mindfully upon my experiences allows me to see them as a collection of intentional decisions rather than a road map to some predetermined destination. Reflection has allowed me to renew my gratitude for the blessings of the journey and to help me leave the destination to the real Driver. When I let go, I receive in return the ability to live fully, gracefully, and intentionally in *this* moment, open to going to the next place my compass will point me.

**Spiritual Principle: Purpose**

"Why aren't you married?" Most single people would be appalled if anyone dares to ask this question! For some, this question may evoke painful memories of a past relationship, call attention to personal issues that we aren't ready to face, or leave the impression that we are somehow "less than" our married counterparts, no matter how great our lives may be.

I was certainly taken aback when my nephew asked this question during a trip to my parents' home for the holidays. I suspect he overheard my sister and me talking about an upcoming wedding, and he was curious about why it wasn't mine. Considering he was only seven at the time, I decided to ask a few clarifying questions:

"Do you think I should be married?"

"Oh, yes!"

"Who do you think I should marry?"

"A boy, of course!"

"What kind of boy?"

"Uh...an older one!"

"How old?"

"Well, he has to be at least fourteen or maybe fifteen."

William put to rest any pressure I felt about getting hit with questions about being single, and for the remainder of my time at home, I had a good story that reminded me to keep a sense of humor about our single lives!

William brings up an important question: Why *aren't* you married? Have you ever stopped to think about this? We assume this question is a criticism of our current situation, but try turning it around: Why *are* you single? Is there a greater goal at work in your life? Do you think God has a purpose for your singleness?

Many people haven't stopped to think about this. When I was in my early twenties, I thought that the purpose of being single meant dedicating time to my career while waiting for Prince Charming to waltz into my life. Then, with marriage in hand and career on track, life could really begin. It didn't take me long to realize that life doesn't happen this way!

Being single means more than waiting to fall in love. For those who genuinely feel called to the sacrament of marriage, the single years can be a great time to prepare for the demands and challenges of a life together. This means more than sitting around waiting for the phone to ring or spending countless hours browsing through online dating profiles. Some of the happiest single people I know are those who are able to reimagine their lives filled with faith, purpose, and passion. They see themselves as complete people, surrounded with love, gratitude, and possibility. While maintaining an essential quality of openness, they understand that romance, dating, and finding a life partner are only one piece of the puzzle.

Our single years are a gift. When we are able to see the purpose in singleness, it is easier to stay present to the moment right in front of us. What is the gift that God wants to give you during this time? What is God asking you to do or accomplish or become? Being single affords us ample amounts of time to pursue a career, develop new friendships, devote time to family, travel to places we've never been, cultivate our relationship skills, volunteer, dedicate time to prayer, and invest in hobbies we enjoy. None of these is dependent upon whether or not we are dating someone.

If I desire to fall in love, I might reflect on how I am being a loving person with the people who are already in my life, with friends, coworkers, family, and my faith community. If what I truly desire is the opportunity to share my joy of travel, cooking, music, or sports with someone special, I might consider the opportunities I already have to engage in these activities and be attentive to the people who also share these interests. If there is an area of my life in need of healing or forgiveness, I should ask God to show me where to find the resources I need to address the difficulties of the past.

The question, "What is the reason for my being here?" may be difficult to answer, especially for those who have a deep and genuine desire to be married or to have children. At times it may feel like those dreams are being withheld, and no amount of prayer or patience can compensate for it. Ask yourself, "What is beneath that longing? How is God cultivating those gifts in my life right now?" And be honest with God about your desires and how you feel—even if you are feeling angry, impatient, rejected, or alone. When we name our deepest desires and truly open ourselves to receiving the gifts God wants to give, we become less concerned with the means by which God chooses to deliver them. Perhaps God is inviting you to look at that desire in a new way.

God has great things in store for us whether we are married or single. When we are so focused on what we hope our lives will become in the future, we may miss the gifts and opportunities available to us in the present. As we grow in appreciation for our single lives, when we are met with the question, "Why aren't you married?" we can respond with all the wonderful things God has in store for us right now.

**Scripture to Remember**

For surely I know the plans I have for you, says the Lord, plans for your welfare and not for harm, to give you a future with hope. (Jeremiah 29:11)

But, as it is written, "What no eye has seen, nor ear heard, nor the human heart conceived, what God has prepared for those who love him." (1 Corinthians 2:9)

I came that they may have life, and have it abundantly. (John 10:10)

**For Reflection**

1. What were my hopes and dreams for the future as I was growing up? How have these plans changed over the years?
2. What is my greatest desire in life right now? What is God's deepest desire for me as a single person?
3. What is my reason for being here? Is there a purpose to being single?

## CHAPTER TWO

# Living Single With **Humility**

*I almost married a guy who was* very *wrong for me because I thought I wasn't me without him. Today, my actual marriage is humorously independent, and we are healthy, happy, and deeply in love. Neither of us needs the other to make us whole and that is what allowed us to fall in love.*—Jenny, 32

## Combating Single Myth #2: **Marriage Equals Wholeness**

One of the sappiest movie lines of all time is a reference to the romantic comedy *Jerry Maguire*, when Jerry says to Dorothy, "You complete me." That one famous line has convinced men and women alike that once we have found that special someone, our other half, our lives will be complete and we will never experience emptiness or loneliness again. We all know that life isn't so picture perfect, but oh, how the movies make us think that real life should be a portrayal of the Hollywood screen!

Likewise, Internet dating sites and singles services are built on the premise that something is missing in our lives, and they make us believe that singles are incomplete without a mate. Television shows like *The Bachelor* and *The Bachelorette* further commercialize the dating process, by trying to sell us the lie that falling in love is a game in which some lucky contestant walks away with the guy or girl of her or his dreams. We use phrases such as "two halves make a whole" and hear people refer to their significant other as "my better half." No wonder single people are often left with the perception that we are somehow not on a par with those who have already found their match.

So many people view marriage as a requirement to attain happiness. Being an integrated, whole person is not dependent on being connected to someone else. I can be fulfilled in or out of a relationship. I can also be broken or unhealthy (emotionally or physically) whether I am in a relationship or not. We each bring our personal histories with us wherever we go. If you are not happy on your own, chances are, it is going to take more than a relationship to resolve your discontent.

We live in a couples' world. But it is not God's plan for everyone to marry or for everyone to have children. It is enough to be single and not to be waiting for something or someone else to "complete" you. We can each be a complete person on our own. Even more, it is necessary to see ourselves as wholly formed individuals if we want to give ourselves fully to a relationship with someone else. When you finally meet the man or woman of your dreams, it will happen on God's time, not your own. Until then, the challenge is to see our relationships as an outcome of sharing the fullness of our lives with others. Rather than viewing romance as a means to wholeness or happiness, it is about moving forward with the life God has called us to live right now.

**Moving Forward:::** *Mary Danek*

As a new teacher, fresh out of college, I often thought, "Where am I going, and why haven't I met anyone yet?" Two of my sisters had married their college sweethearts. My cool, single sister was living in the city. Another sister had married and quickly divorced. My youngest sister was engaged and headed in a direction I wished was mine. Of my four brothers, one was divorced and one was engaged. Why did it feel like my clock was ticking? What was the point of being single?

I was living at home and saving money, but "for what?," I sometimes thought. I enjoyed teaching but couldn't help thinking, "What's next and when is it coming?" I worked hard and felt like I had a purpose, and I was beginning to see my true talents. I trusted that God had a plan for me, but I largely thought that it was for me to meet someone. God had his own plan in mind.

After my first year of teaching, a friend asked if I would be interested in traveling. We decided to spend a month backpacking through Europe. It was there that I began to see who I truly was, and for the first time I came to know my single self. I felt free from my routine, and my set place in life. Every cathedral and square we walked into only reinforced the beauty and mystery of God and all creation. I was in awe to be a part of what God had made.

Two weeks into the trip my bag was stolen. I spent the day crying, after losing everything valuable. My friend asked, "Do you want to go home?" I did, but my answer came, "No, I want to stay." I needed to finish this part of the journey. I will never doubt what God had planned all along. I came home from that trip knowing exactly where I was headed—*forward.* One year after that trip I met my future husband. Meeting him didn't fill a void, it only added to my life and to me.

Someone once said to me, "Don't worry when you fall, at least you know you're still moving forward." Being single isn't about being alone. It is a chance to be your true self, moving forward, and understanding what you can do. Accepting God's path is a great challenge, staying on it even greater. I couldn't see the path when I was on it as a single person. As I look back, I realize that my journey unfolded just as God wanted, and I trust that I am still on it.

I believe in the strength of the Holy Family, and I often pray to the Blessed Mother Mary to help me accept this path I am on. As a single woman, I prayed for strength and understanding. As a married woman, I pray for guidance. Mary accepted God's path for her life even though she didn't fully understand it. So too will the path of all single people become clear as they accept and trust in God's love, understanding, forgiveness, and direction in all parts of their life.

**Spiritual Principle: Humility**

When you think of the word *humility*, who is the first person that comes to mind?

Many of us associate humility with someone like Bl. Mother Teresa. A woman of great integrity and deep spirituality, she founded her own religious order, the Missionaries of Charity, who dedicate their lives to serving the poorest of the poor. Even after winning the Nobel Peace Prize in 1979, Mother Teresa continued to live a simple lifestyle, maintained few possessions, and cared for the sick and dying until her own death in 1997.

I can name many people who embody humility. Some less famous folks who come to mind include my dentist, a favorite professor, our church pianist, and a computer engineer with whom I used to work. They are all people who are comfortable in their own skin. Each of them is well educated in their particular field of study and successful in different ways. They have no need to make a big impression on anyone else, yet time and again I find myself in awe of what they do. Humble people exude confidence and success without being pompous about it. They attract like-minded people with a similar zeal for life and passion for their particular cause.

Often humility is misrepresented as a quality of those who see themselves as small or insignificant or attempt to place themselves beneath others. As the popular saying goes, "Humble people don't think less of themselves; they just think of themselves less." Those who are humble have no need to brag, but likewise, they don't waste time trying to hide their accomplishments. They are proud of their successes without being arrogant. Humble people are often described as "genuine," and they come across as "real" people. The root of the word *humility* (from the Latin *humus*) means to be grounded or from the earth. Humility is to know who we are and who we are not.

Twentieth-century spiritual writer and Trappist monk Thomas Merton writes,

> [H]umility consists in being precisely the person you actually are before God, and since no two people are alike, if you have the humility to be yourself you will not be like anyone else in the whole universe. But this individuality will not necessarily assert itself on the surface of everyday life. It will not be a matter of mere appearances, or opinions, or tastes, or ways of doing things. It is something deep in the soul.[1]

Who am I in the eyes of God? What does God see that no one else sees? This is humility. We achieve humility when we speak the truth of who we are with our lives, when the person you are internally is congruent to the person others see and experience externally. Humility is about recognizing our gifts, letting them shine, giving thanks to God who gives them to us, and sharing them with the rest of the world.

There is something incredibly liberating about being yourself. God gives each of us the freedom to be who we are. I don't have to filter who I am or the things I love about myself in order to fit someone else's expectations. It is OK to have my own identity, my own friends, my own thoughts and feelings. I can think and feel differently from others. Humility is about knowing ourselves, what makes us tick, what sets us off, and what our likes and dislikes are. As we come to accept ourselves for who we are, we are naturally equipped to accept other people for who they are.

Humility is a characteristic toward which all of us should strive. Single people in particular can benefit from the lessons of humility, especially when we are confronted with expectations about how our lives "should be" or find ourselves dissatisfied with the direction in which our lives are headed. Some of the most content single people I know are those who, with great humility, have accepted that being single is OK. They may even have a sense of humor about it without resorting to self-deprecating comments or disparaging remarks about others.

When we embrace humility, we are able to find joy in every stage of life. I can go through life complaining, comparing myself to others, or resenting those who are in a romantic relationship. Or, I can embrace my singleness with all of its lessons, challenges, blessings, and opportunities. I may not always like being single, and there are some things I cannot change about it, but I can control my attitude and approach to it.

The key to a fulfilling single life is to believe that I can be a complete person on my own. It is enough to be single and not waiting for another to complete me. This time in your life gives you the opportunity to find out who you are, what you really love about yourself, and what you want to become. As we humbly accept the gift of being single, we are able to move forward with full and abundant lives.

**Scripture to Remember**

He has told you, O mortal, what is good;
and what does the LORD require of you
but to do justice, and to love kindness,
and to walk humbly with your God? (Micah 6:8)

I therefore, the prisoner in the Lord, beg you to lead a life worthy of the calling to which you have been called, with all humility and gentleness, with patience, bearing with one another in love... (Ephesians 4:1–2)

You are the light of the world. A city built on a hill cannot be hid. No one after lighting a lamp puts it under the bushel basket, but on the lampstand, and it gives light to all in the house. In the same way, let your light shine before others, so that they may see your good works and give glory to your Father in heaven. (Matthew 5:14–16)

**For Reflection**

1. Who in my life exemplifies humility? What characteristics about these people do I wish to embody?
2. What does God see in me that others do not see? How can I allow these qualities to shine?
3. What prevents me from being my truest self?

# CHAPTER THREE

## Living Single With **Wisdom**

*For years my Mom was concerned about how I would eat! "How are you going to get dinner tonight?" was a common question when we would talk on my drive home. Now, I'm actually recognized as the best cook in the family, and I have introduced Mom to spices and Thai food.* –John, 34

### Combating Single Myth #3: **You're Not an Adult Until You Are Married**

Do you remember the age at which you realized that you were no longer a kid? Sometime in my early twenties, I became consciously aware that I was no longer an adolescent, but I didn't exactly feel like a grown-up. Traditionally, adulthood is marked by high school or college graduation, marriage, home ownership, financial independence, having children, and career advancement. For many people today, however, the traditional milestones happen later, occur in a different order, or are skipped all together.

Single people in particular are challenged to rethink these milestones and the markers of adulthood. Adulthood is defined by age, but it is also characterized by the moments that catapult us into maturity, the instances when we are forced to make adult decisions or take on increasing responsibilities. I feel just a little bit older every time my car breaks down, when I go to the hardware store to buy supplies for a do-it-yourself project, and when the last of my college loans is finally paid!

Similarly, traditional gender expectations, the ways we think of men and women as adults, have begun to shift. Unlike previous generations, women are taught to be strong, independent self-starters, and it is not unheard of for men to carry some domestic responsibilities. There are women who manage their own investments and gladly do their own taxes. I know men who buy groceries, enjoy cooking, and do their own laundry. Many single people, whether they rent or own, have a place that they call "home" where friends and family regularly gather.

It can be discouraging when we recognize that single people are subjected to different expectations than our married friends or family members, especially if those expectations place us in a position of lesser importance or devalue our contribution. This happens when singles are passed over for certain opportunities, when people make assumptions about our financial priorities, or when the opinion of our married siblings carries more weight in family matters.

For some people, marriage is the ultimate mark of adulthood. It is proof that you have arrived in the world of grown-ups and are ready to take on important new responsibilities.

**The Christmas Invitation:::**

*Beth M. Knobbe*

Last December I received an invitation from my aunt for the annual potluck Christmas party for our extended family of aunts, uncles, cousins, their spouses, and children. The invitation went something like this:

> You are cordially invited to our Annual Christmas Party on the evening of December 25. Festivities will begin at 6:00 PM at our home. Please bring a dish to share.

My aunt then included a list of what everyone was expected to bring. Aunt Margie always makes salad and my great aunt Anne always brings potatoes. Then came this stinger, "The married cousins are asked to bring an appetizer, snack, or a bottle of wine to share."

I was dumbfounded. The *married* cousins are asked to bring something? As if being married suddenly qualifies you to cook or select a good bottle of wine? I'm sure what she really meant is that the *adult* cousins were invited to bring a dish.

I read the invitation again. It was pretty clear. Not only did it say "married" cousins, but my aunt even listed their names: Jenny, Lisa, Ashley, Bridget, and so on. Worse yet, she only listed the women! Ashley is married to my cousin Steve, and Lisa is married to my cousin Greg.

In that moment, I was consciously aware of the generation gap that exists in our family. Just because my single cousins Michael (divorced), Erica (seriously dating someone), and I (single) are all in our early thirties, we shouldn't be disqualified from fully participating in our family traditions.

I was also consciously aware of the false expectations heaped upon us by our parents' generation: first, that you're not an adult until you're married; second, that women are solely responsible for preparing the party food.

I spent a long time thinking about how to respond, and I finally called my mom for advice. She hadn't noticed the "married cousins" comment on the invitation, but she immediately sensed my discomfort, affirming what I knew deep down but wasn't ready to admit: This wasn't about who was bringing the potatoes. It was about being accepted as part of the family. "I'm sure you could bring something to the party," she said, "and anything you bring would be appreciated, but what we really want for Christmas is *you*."

The same day I received the family Christmas invitation, I attended the most wonderful holiday party hosted by my friend John. In a room full of thirty-somethings, women and men, most of whom are single, we were treated to amazing food, great wine, and fabulous company. A fun night out with friends and a long conversation with my mom was everything I needed to be reminded that I am accepted and loved regardless of my single status.

**Spiritual Principle: Wisdom**

How many of us find ourselves, literally or figuratively, still seated at the "kids' table" during family gatherings? Being recognized as a full-grown member of the family requires a shift in perspective and making a conscious choice to act differently by offering to bring a favorite dish, taking a turn at the grill, or arriving early to set the table or arrange chairs. Holidays in particular can be tough for single people. I am sometimes jealous of my siblings who are married and are creating traditions with their kids that are unique to their nuclear family. How do you celebrate the holidays with your family and friends? Are there new traditions that you can create because they are important to you?

One mark of maturity is wisdom. Wisdom is more than growing old or increasing in age or passing years. Wisdom is measured by more than our intellectual capacity or academic degrees. It is more than acquiring street smarts in order to survive. Our hearts derive wisdom from reflecting on our experiences, acknowledging our feelings, responding to love, extending forgiveness, and being attentive to the ways our hearts have been broken. Wisdom is about what we bring to the situation.

We each bring the whole of our experiences. Wisdom asks, "What have I learned? How do I become better and not bitter?" Wisdom does not equate to playing it safe all the time. We become wise when we take risks, knowing that we may get hurt or we may discover tremendous joy. We become wise when we allow ourselves to be surprised by God's goodness, to take time to celebrate our accomplishments and give thanks for the gifts in our lives. It takes a certain amount of wisdom to reflect on our single years and say, "I'm OK with the place where I am right now."

The book of Sirach tells us that wisdom comes from the fear of the Lord (1:12). Do I stand in awe of God and recognize God's divine providence guiding in my life? Perhaps God has some greater purpose in mind for my single years? It is a time for learning and growth, and it is also a time to become wise in the ways of the heart.

**Scripture to Remember**

And this is my prayer, that your love may overflow more and more with knowledge and full insight to help you to determine what is best, so that in the day of Christ you may be pure and blameless. (Philippians 1:9–10)

For wisdom is more mobile than any motion;
because of her pureness she pervades and penetrates all things.
For she is a breath of the power of God,
and a pure emanation of the glory of the Almighty;
therefore nothing defiled gains entrance into her.
For she is a reflection of eternal light,
a spotless mirror of the working of God,
and an image of his goodness.
Although she is but one, she can do all things,

and while remaining in herself, she renews all things;
in every generation she passes into holy souls
and makes them friends of God, and prophets;
for God loves nothing so much as the person who lives with wisdom. (Wisdom 7:24–28)

Who is wise and understanding among you? Show by your good life that your works are done with gentleness born of wisdom. But if you have bitter envy and selfish ambition in your hearts, do not be boastful and false to the truth. But the wisdom from above is first pure, then peaceable, gentle, willing to yield, full of mercy and good fruits, without a trace of partiality or hypocrisy. (James 3:13–14, 17)

**For Reflection**

1. When have I felt snubbed or slighted because of my single status? How did that experience make me feel and how did I respond? How do I continue to grow in maturity without becoming cynical or hard-hearted?
2. What have been the markers of adulthood for me, when I knew that I had arrived in the world of adults? How have I celebrated those accomplishments?
3. What does it mean for me to be wise? How do I share the wisdom of age and experience with those around me?

# CHAPTER FOUR

## Living Single With **Gratitude**

*Miss Kim, what's your boyfriend's name? I mean, you aren't married, so you have to have a boyfriend, right?* —Kim, third grade teacher

### Combating Single Myth #4: **Singles Want to be Set-up**

"You're such a pretty girl, why aren't you dating anyone?" This was the greeting I received from my uncle for what seemed like the third holiday in a row. Picking up, as if on cue, my cousin began telling me about a recent law school graduate who was working in his office. "He's a really nice guy. I'll give him your phone number." My single status quickly developed into the central plotline of the conversation before I even had a chance to set down my dinner plate. By the time dessert was served, they had devised a strategic plan for finding my future husband.

Although they mean well, it can be incredibly awkward when friends want to set us up. Even worse is the pressure from family members for you to find a mate, make your way down the aisle, and provide grandchildren before it's too late. How do you respond when you become a target for such unwanted advances? Do you take people's unsolicited advice, trust your own instincts, or quickly change the subject?

Despite the best intentions of the giver, I generally find that unsolicited advice tends to backfire. Instead of lifting my spirits, it only serves to remind me that I've not found someone on my own. I already contend with my own feelings of inadequacy on occasion. Having my mom, dad, siblings, or friends trying to "fix the situation" seems to imply that my own approach to the single life isn't working. Sometimes I want to scream, "My life isn't broken!" Being single isn't a problem that needs to be "solved" or an issue that needs to be "fixed." For me and for many singles, we just wish our families would see it this way.

**Why Can't You Find a Nice Catholic Boy?::: ***Sarah Coles*

I'll never forget it. It was Good Friday, 2003. I was just twenty-one years old, not an Old Maid by any stretch. But my mother, in an attempt to do, well, whatever it is that mothers do, thought that I needed to find myself a good Catholic boy. We were on an afternoon pilgrimage in downtown New Orleans visiting churches and walking the Stations of the Cross. What better place to meet a son-in-law, right? About half way through, we grew hot and tired, so her mind and eyes started wandering. Soon she picked a nice looking guy, made a plan, and started talking to him. I simply rolled my eyes and tried to pretend this wasn't happening. We soon found out this nice young man was studying to become a priest. That's right, my mother attempted to set me up with a seminarian!

I often think back to that day and wonder, "What was my mom thinking?" Did she find it strange that I rarely went out on dates? Had I recently complained about loneliness? Or was she simply bored? I suppose it could have been any or all of the above. Eight years later, I'm still single. And although she has not recently attempted any amusing set-ups, I think my mom still worries.

But do I worry? I don't know; that's kind of a tough one to answer. For the most part, I typically see myself as a strong-willed, self-sufficient woman. I have great friends, a job I love, and tons of fun in my free time. I'm free to travel whenever I want, never have to ask permission to splurge on something nice, and I'm not responsible for anyone beside myself and my cat. But I can't seem to scratch that itching feeling in the back of my heart that I'm missing out on something wonderful.

I attribute part of it to the fact that in the past few years I've watched one friend after another get married and start a family. It's actually quite amusing to open up my Facebook account and look at the most recent stories. At least half of the news items include pictures of someone's wedding, ultrasound or new baby, and status updates about their incredible partner, fiancé, spouse, or child.

I'm sure another part of my discontent is the combination of my ticking biological clock and the questioning looks I get from my family. Most recently my grandfather asked me, at the Christmas dinner table no less, when I would be providing him with great-grandkids. Thanks, Grandpa! No pressure there!

Aside from those moments of doubt about the future of my marital and parental status, I love my life. I love my independence, and I love my family and friends. In moments of doubt I try to rely on my faith to guide my heart. I know that I am doing great stuff with my life, and what I am doing now will lead to great things in the future. All of this has been guided by the Holy Spirit. As I reflect on the path that led me here, I cannot help but notice God's hand in every step along the way. Would God's hand have been just as present had I made different decisions? Of course! But, together God and I have brought me to this place. Together God and I will take me where I need to be in the future.

Perhaps, in the end, I'm touched that my mom tried to find me a boyfriend, seminarian or not! And perhaps I secretly hope she will try again. I trust that with or without that perfect match, I will still know happiness and peace.

**Spiritual Principle: Gratitude**

Who among us hasn't railed against an overbearing mother, a meddlesome aunt, or a scrutinizing big sister? Especially when it comes to their questions about who we are dating, when the family gets to meet him/her, or the not-so-subtle reminder about wanting grandchildren?

I recently received an invitation to a dinner party hosted by my friend Susan. When I asked if I could bring anything, she responded, "Are you dating anyone? You're welcome to bring a guest." There was a time when I would have been up in arms over such a response. All I wanted to bring was a loaf of fresh bread or bottle of wine. How dare she suggest that I need to bring a date! Instead, knowing Susan (a strong independent woman who chose to marry later in life), and recalling many wonderful conversations about the value of our single lives, I realized that her invitation was simply that—an invitation, not a judgment.

I found myself grateful for the invitation. I suspect this was Susan's way of saying, "You are worthy of a companion. We'd like to get to know your friends. We enjoy your company, and we hope there are other people in your life (perhaps even a significant someone) who might have the pleasure of your company, too."

It's easy to extend the benefit of the doubt or offer a word of thanks to a supportive friend who understands our situation. It's not quite as easy when Aunt Sally drops admonishing remarks like, "It just hurts your mother so much to see you single." How can I take this as a compliment and not a criticism of my single status? Such comments raise doubt and worry in our own minds. Am I in the right place? Will I be taken care of? And what if I never find that special someone?

Our ability to give thanks and express our gratitude to God for all that has been given to us brings with it the contentment and peace that many singles seek. When we approach life with a sense of gratitude for all things, no matter how big or small, it gives us the ability to cherish the present moment, even if it is different than the ideal picture in our mind.

Gratitude opens us to the infinite capacity to love. Being grateful for the blessings in my life helps me to focus more on the things I have and worry less about the things that I do not have. Gratitude strengthens my trust in God that I will be taken care of, instead of evaluating my life against those who seem to have everything or more of the things I desire. When I pause to give thanks, I know there will be enough, and I am not lacking in anything.

During his late thirties, when uncertain about whether or not marriage was in his future, my friend Joe spent a day with his brother's wife and children. While getting ready to take the kids to the park, his sister-in-law asked, "Will you tie Caroline's shoes?" On any other day Joe would have wasted time worrying and wondering about why he hadn't met someone as equally great as his sister-in-law. Instead, he tells me, "When I bent down to tie my niece's shoes, I found myself staring into the same big brown eyes that my brothers and I all share. In that moment, I was overwhelmed with gratitude for Caroline's presence in my life. I am proud to be her uncle and cherish the fun times we have together. I whispered a prayer of thanks to God, and any lingering sense of jealousy quickly faded."

Gratitude points the way toward what is most important in life. It helps clarify the things we truly desire and seek in a relationship. Gratitude helps me see that my parents want the best for me, even if their hopes for grandchildren are not consistent with my current reality. Gratitude helps me understand the difference between my own desires and people who project their desires onto me. Ultimately, gratitude shows me where love *is* present in my life: where intimacy resides in my relationships, where laughter overflows in my friendships, and how the generosity of friends and strangers alike provides for what otherwise seems to be missing.

During a particularly difficult time, I decided to keep a gratitude journal. At the end of each day, I wrote down three things for which I could give thanks. Looking back at the entries, I see hopeful messages: I am grateful for the kindness of a coworker, a long conversation with one of my students, and hearing someone affirm, "You're really good at what you do." I was reminded that there will be good days and bad days, average days and extraordinary days. My single status doesn't cause them to occur or increase their frequency.

Finally, gratitude is one of those gifts that replenishes itself. One of the fruits of gratitude is generosity. When we are grateful and trust that God will provide everything we need, we are more eager to share our gifts with others—from material gifts, to our gift of time, and our ability to listen and be present with others. As grateful people give more, they also recognize the gifts received in return. When we carry a spirit of gratitude, everyone around us benefits.

**Scripture to Remember**

It is good to give thanks to the Lord,
to sing praises to your name, O Most High;
to declare your steadfast love in the morning,
and your faithfulness by night... (Psalm 92:1–2)

Do not worry about anything, but in everything by prayer and supplication with thanksgiving let your requests be made known to God. (Philippians 4:6)

Rejoice always, pray without ceasing, give thanks in all circumstances; for this is the will of God in Christ Jesus for you. Do not quench the Spirit. Do not despise the words of prophets, but test everything; hold fast to what is good; abstain from every form of evil. (1 Thessalonians 5:16–22)

**For Reflection**

1. How do I respond to friends or family who inquire about my relationship status or insist on setting me up on dates? How do I put their concerns into perspective?
2. I will list three things for which I am most grateful today. I may choose to start small: good health, warm sunshine, gainful employment. What do the items on my gratitude list say about my values and priorities in life?
3. Consider a time when being single has been difficult. How has God provided for me during challenging times? What have I learned and how have I grown as a result of that experience?

CHAPTER FIVE

# Living Single With **Forgiveness**

*Mature people apologize explicitly, and we become mature by apologizing.* —Ronald Rolheiser[1]

## Combating Single Myth #5: **Single People Have "Issues"**

The play, *Almost, Maine,* by John Cariani features a cast of quirky characters in the fictitious town of unincorporated "Almost" in northern Maine. Beneath a backdrop of falling snow and the northern lights, eccentric couples in long wool skirts and quilted plaid vests take their place on the stage; and with dry humor and witty drama, they stage nine short stories about life, love, and being human.

One of the vignettes features Phil and Marci, who have just spent an uncomfortable evening together at the ice skating rink. Sitting on a park bench before returning to their car, Marci discovers that she has misplaced one of her shoes. Meanwhile, their conversation follows along these lines. "What's wrong?" "Nothing." "Are you mad?" "No, I'm not mad!"

Marci scrambles to find her missing footwear, hobbling across the stage with a shoe on one foot and an ice skate on the other. Following close behind, Phil asks again, "Are you sure you're not mad at me?" They have clearly become emotionally detached from one another, and the lost shoe quickly becomes a metaphor for everything that seems to be missing from their relationship.

Finally, Marci blurts out, "Happy Anniversary!" This is the final straw. It is their anniversary, and Phil has forgotten. As Marci prepares to storm off the stage, a single shoe drops from the ceiling and lands with a resounding thud.

How often do we find ourselves waiting for the other shoe to drop? We meet someone special but then begin to second guess why a person who is so funny, good looking, or successful is not in a committed relationship with someone else. Along with that missing shoe, we begin to wonder what kind of baggage is hiding in the closet. Perhaps there was a relationship that ended badly, poor social skills, unresolved anger, or hidden financial troubles. We insist that there must be something wrong with this person, who otherwise seems so right.

The more unsettling realization comes when we dare to ask, "Is there something wrong with *me*?" We all have our bad habits, quirky behaviors, or a tendency to put up our defenses from time to time. We all have situations from our past (or the present) which we don't like to discuss. One of the biggest risks of being in a relationship is trusting that I will be accepted and loved for all that I bring and all that seems to be missing. The single years are an opportune time to take care of our personal baggage and unresolved hurts from the past. It is impossible to move forward with our dreams for the future, unless we understand exactly what is holding us back and learn to love our single selves.

**Learning to Love the Single Me:::** *Mike Hayes*

"If only I were married, things would be perfect!" Anyone married is laughing at that sentence—not because we're dissatisfied with our significant others, or even because time eroded our starry-eyed romantic notions of love, but because we know that we married someone whom we love, not someone who has to meet all of our expectations.

I wake up each day knowing that my wife will not meet my expectations of who I think she should be. And she doesn't have to, because she is not the person I constructed for myself. She is Marion, my wife, and I fell in love with her, not my idea of what a wife should be. Together we know that our ability to love one another through our imperfections has ultimately drawn us closer. This has become for us the backbone of a committed marriage.

I used to utter that infamous "if only" phrase as well. What I, as a single person, needed to embrace was the idea of being loved for who I really am. Many of my relationships developed into something deeper, but often they resulted in people not accepting me, or I found myself trying to change in order to measure up to their ideal. Every breakup came with the feeling that some part of me was unlovable, like I was never a "perfect match" for anyone.

The idea of not being in a committed relationship also brought great anxiety, and fear often kept me in bad relationships. It was easier to stay attached than to risk rejection and being alone. But being alone is where I was called to be, allowing me to get in touch with my true self. I was able to discern who I was and where God was calling me in my chosen vocation, and also to discern what kind of marriage and partner I wanted. I needed a woman who could see me for who I really am and be proud of me and not try to "train me" or "fix me."

But first, I had to be proud of "the single me." I was trying too hard in a career that didn't fulfill my desires. I often tried to impress people. It was only when I could feel more comfortable and confident with myself that I could ever really attract that "right" person. I knew the love of my life would fall in love with the real me. I wanted someone else to love that person as much as I do.

Looking back, the staleness and the pain of loss were the result of others trying to love an incomplete person, someone not ready to be loved. When those losses subsided, however, the real blessing of my life was the opportunity to deeply look at myself and to develop into a person who was self-confident and mature. It was during that single period that I truly enjoyed meeting myself. Only when I truly knew myself could I ever look at other people and accept them.

The truth is that we need to get past our pain and anxiety, our insecurities and embarrassments, and accept the cross of who we are. If someone else is going to love us, they need to love our deepest self, the unmasked reality of who we are. What is it in our own feelings about ourselves that needs to die in order for us to rise again to a new and better acceptance of our lives where we live forever confident in ourselves and without fear of rejection?

God knows that we aren't perfect. Can we trust that the person God sees within us is beautiful enough for anyone? We need to. If we truly become who God has created us to be, then it doesn't matter if someone else sees us as lovable or not. What matters is that we can love ourselves as God does. And that should be more than enough for everyone.

### Spiritual Principle: Forgiveness

None of us wants to be that cynical single person who goes through life with a jaded outlook on the world. Yet sometimes life throws things our way, and we want nothing more than to dive into a drinking binge or camp out in front of the television with a sappy movie and a pint of chocolate ice cream. Much to our chagrin, sometimes our best response to a crisis is to throw ourselves a pity party and invite all our friends!

Maybe you are someone who forgives easily and has moved forward with few regrets from the past. Most of us do not need to look far to discover our share of mistakes, missteps, and ungraceful moments. Perhaps we carry the consequences of an abusive parent, a debilitating injury, an unexpected layoff, unresolved grief, or a broken engagement. The emotional strain can linger long after the physical effects have subsided, and regret can take its toll for a few weeks or haunt us for years.

Just as our unresolved hurts are usually long-lasting and complex, forgiveness is not simple nor is it easy. Sometimes our tendency is to avoid pain, shut the door on the past, and pretend bad things didn't happen. Forgiveness does not mean that we simply forget. True forgiveness requires that we first acknowledge that we've been offended. I don't deny my actions, or what the other person did, or pretend it wasn't wrong. As difficult as this exercise may be, forgiveness begins when we are able to honestly name the injury that has been done to us or the pain we have caused another person or ourselves. Healing comes when we are able to name our ailments, claim our broken hearts or bruised ego, and envision our future as not defined by our past.

There may come a time when we need to ask forgiveness from those we've hurt or from those who have hurt us, knowing that sometimes a face-to-face apology is too risky or even impossible. However, apologizing doesn't reestablish the relationship, and saying "I'm sorry" doesn't mean that we have to be best friends. Rather, forgiveness relinquishes us from the need to hold a grudge against the other person. It gives us permission to let go of our desire to get even, and it allows us to unleash the ball and chain that weighs down our hearts. Forgiveness invites us to see this person as someone just like us—someone who is imperfect, someone who was responding out of their own brokenness or weakness, and someone who God loves despite their failures and shortcomings.

Often the person who is most in need of forgiveness is me. Forgiveness ultimately requires us to see ourselves as God sees us—as the apple of God's eye, as someone who is loved and treasured, deserving of God's mercy, and worthy of God's forgiveness. We must give ourselves permission to learn from our mistakes, and then move on with our lives. Sometime forgiveness is both about acknowledging what we did wrong and accepting that God still loves us in spite of all this. God loves us for who we are and gives us the courage to change. When we are able to love the "real me" and accept our own idiosyncrasies, we unconsciously give others permission to do the same.

No one is perfect. We don't easily let go of the past, and it takes time to reestablish trust with others, with God, and within ourselves. The sacrament of reconciliation is a powerful tool in growing toward wholeness again. Just as sin separates us from both God and neighbor, reconciliation restores our relationship with both God and the community. Reconciliation is a place where we can let go of the past, experience God's mercy, and move forward with God's grace. Ultimately, it is God who forgives. When we allow our faults and imperfections to be heard and received by another human being, we open ourselves to accept God's unconditional mercy, forgiveness, and love.

Forgiveness is at the heart of all good relationships, whether that relationship is with a significant someone, a good friend, a sibling, a coworker, a neighbor, or the relationship we have with ourselves. It is important to remember that forgiveness takes practice and patience. And forgiveness is a process; it is not something that happens overnight. However, as we make forgiveness a habit in our day-to-day lives, we find that we are no longer weighed down by the mistakes of the past and open ourselves to all the possibilities of the future. It is something we are always working on, and we hope always getting better at doing, as we learn to love our single selves.

**Scripture to Remember**

But this is the covenant that I will make with the house of Israel after those days, says the Lord: I will put my law within them, and I will write it on their hearts; and I will be their God, and they shall be my people. No longer shall they teach one another, or say to each other, "Know the Lord," for they shall all know me, from the least of them to the greatest, says the Lord; for I will forgive their iniquity, and remember their sin no more. (Jeremiah 31:33–34)

But I say to you that listen, love your enemies, do good to those who hate you, bless those who curse you, pray for those who abuse you. If anyone strikes you on the cheek, offer the other also; and from anyone who takes away your coat do not withhold even your shirt. Give to everyone who begs from you; and if anyone takes away your goods, do not ask for them again. Do to others as you would have them do to you. (Luke 6:27–31)

Jesus straightened up and said to her, "Woman, where are they? Has no one condemned you?" She said, "No one, sir." And Jesus said, "Neither do I condemn you. Go your way, and from now on do not sin again." (John 8:10–11)

**For Reflection**

1. Are there people in my life who I need to forgive? Where do I hold on to anger, jealousy, or resentment? What is one step I can take toward forgiveness?
2. What qualities about myself are hardest to accept? Are there things that I've done that I am not proud of? Where do I need to forgive myself?

3. Do I believe that God loves me as I am? Do I trust that God's abundant mercy and unconditional forgiveness is always available to me? Is there anything holding me back from my relationship with God?

## CHAPTER SIX

# Living Single With **Discernment**

*There is only one vocation. Whether you teach or live in the cloister or nurse the sick, whether you are in religion or out of it, married or single, no matter who you are or what you are...you are called to a deep interior life.*—Thomas Merton[1]

## Combating Single Myth #6: **All Singles Should Consider Religious Life**

"Are you a sister?"

It seemed like an innocent question, but I knew exactly where the conversation was headed. It was the end of an eight-day silent retreat, and the question was being asked by a woman twice my age wearing a simple skirt and blouse with a modest crucifix dangling from a chain around her neck. I smiled, "No, I'm not a sister, but thank you for asking."

She responded, "Oh, that's too bad. I'm sure you'd make a wonderful sister." The cynical side of me wanted to reply, "How would you know? We just spent eight days together in *silence*!" Instead, I politely thanked her again and assured her that I would pray about it.

I later shared this story with a friend of mine. "Why is it that every year on retreat someone asks if I'm a nun?" I asked her. "And why do I feel guilty having to explain that I'm not?" With a smirk on her face and a twinkle in her eye, my friend offered this simple solution, "Next time, say *yes*. After all, you have four siblings. Of course, you're a sister!"

For the record, I have considered joining a religious community. The fact that I attend daily Mass, make an annual silent retreat, and work for the church is all pretty good evidence that I may be suited to the lifestyle of most religious orders. I've spent a lot of time in prayer and sought input from trusted advisors, and while I have not ruled it out completely, I'm pretty sure it's *not* where God is calling me.

Singles live in this ambiguous space of not knowing who or what comes next. We are called to live in openness and trust with God as the primary partner for deciding how our lives will unfold. Perhaps God *is* calling you to the priesthood or religious life, and for reasons that God only knows, that call is still on hold. The same could be said of marriage. The single life is a great time to learn and practice the tools of discernment—prayerful and intentional decision-making. Ultimately, we can trust that our future is in God's hands, and God is leading us toward that next step whatever it may be.

**Open to the Vocation Question:::** *Julia Benson*

*O Mary, Chosen Spouse of the Holy Spirit, pray for me!* I remember clearly the night God released me from all anxiety surrounding my fear of being called to the religious life. It is a moment of clarity that reminds me that God is present and working in my life even when every sign seems to indicate otherwise.

I was in my early twenties and living on the north side of Chicago. I had just come through a wonderful period during which I was a member of a volunteer community while teaching in an inner-city school on the south side. I loved the intensity of community life, surrounded by individuals who both supported and challenged me, which brought the reality of living as a single person into sharp focus as I transitioned from this environment. As I watched more and more of my friends get married and start families, I began to wonder if and when my turn was going to come. Along with that came the small voice of fear, and I began to question if marriage was really the vocation that I was called to and if perhaps I should be considering other paths.

From time to time I would be asked, "Have you considered the religious life?" This was a good and valid question, when not raised in the context of a conversation about my dating life or lack thereof. The question began to bother me, paradoxically, not because the idea of religious life was not attractive to me, but as I came to understand that I was making the vocation of wife and mother into an idol—one which I was not very willing to let go.

Things came to a head one evening as I lay in bed. I was mightily resisting in my spirit the words that the Lord was trying to speak to me. I could almost hear God saying, "Do not be afraid. I am not asking you to pursue the religious life. I am only asking you to be open to the idea of pursuing the religious life." In that moment of grace, there was an opening, and I gave up the struggle.

"All right!" I shouted at God in my head, "I will be open to considering the religious life." Immediately, I felt the most profound sense of peace and contentment, and I easily fell asleep. From that moment, I felt no further call or desire to pursue a religious vocation.

A few months later, I attended a discernment retreat with an order of Dominican sisters whose charism is attractive to me. On this retreat, I received the Marian prayer, "O Mary, Chosen Spouse of the Holy Spirit, pray for me!" The prayer filled my heart and reminded me that I would be chosen, just as Mary was chosen, not by doing anything extraordinary but by pursuing the life I was called to lead.

God continues to do a great work in me. He has given me time in which I've learned to know and accept myself. He has also healed some of the wounds that kept me from truly being Christ present in the world and from fully opening my heart.

My single years have been full of life, and the moments of loneliness have moved me closer to Christ. I trust that God is still working in my life, and on the good days, I truly believe that he has called me exactly to where I am. In these moments, I embrace my past, my present and all the lessons that lie before me.

**Spiritual Principle: Discernment**

So often, we view the single life as a time of waiting for something better to come along—for the "real call" or our "real vocation." The tools for discernment apply regardless of which path you are leaning toward—marriage, religious life, priesthood, or even accepting the single life as our chosen path. There is no prescribed course for navigating the single life, so discernment becomes an important tool as we make day-to-day decisions and significant life choices.

When it comes to discerning a vocation to religious life, it is important to remember that the call to religious life is precisely that—a *call*. It should not be treated as an obligation made under pressure from those who insist, "But you would make such a good priest (or a good sister)." Likewise, entering seminary or joining a convent is probably not the best decision for someone hoping to escape the difficulties of life or seeking solace after a painful breakup.

Religious life is not the "default option" when other opportunities fail to materialize. Those called to priesthood and religious life have their own distinct role to play within the life of the church, as do those who are married or single. Joining a religious community does not give anyone a special degree of worthiness, and it doesn't make one a "better" Christian. God does not love religious more or less than anyone else, just as being single does not make us less loveable or less spiritual or less holy.

Discernment is particularly challenging when single people have gifts that are legitimately well suited for acceptance into a religious community. Perhaps others recognize the compassion we have for the poor, the generosity with which we share our gifts with the wider community, a desire to connect with God through prayer and contemplation, or a love for the sacraments. Any of those attributes may be a good indicator that we should consider religious life, but none is a guarantee. Can we hear these things and accept them in freedom without putting undue pressure on ourselves to make a decision? Do we allow ourselves to honestly bring these observations into prayer?

One resource to enlist when making important decisions is a spiritual director who can listen with an impartial ear, without any preconceived notions of what our response should or ought to be. By listening without judgment, a spiritual director helps us listen for where God is truly calling us, name our deepest desires and fears, and discern God's call. Spiritual directors urge us to ask for courage to respond and help us distinguish the true voice of God from the sound of our own egos or the voices of family and friends.

Life is always unfinished, and discernment is not a one-time decision. Even for those who take vows in marriage or religious life, the promise of fidelity is just the beginning of a lifetime commitment. The events of ordinary life require ongoing discernment, whether that means responding to changes in our career, prioritizing our volunteer commitments, or resolving a family crisis. Sometimes change rests within our control, while other times it is thrust upon us with little or no warning. None of us ever knows all that God has in store for us.

Just as God has assigned a particular role to the married and the ordained, God has a purpose for those who are single. In many ways, the single life can be our vocation. When we embrace this state in life, with its essential openness and waiting, singles can be a role model for discernment and trust in God. Being single is a call to generosity of time and talent. It is a call to commitment to our community and family in traditional and reimagined ways. God calls us to be ready to respond to God's invitation. For some that may eventually mean a call to marriage or religious life. However, for people who remain single for their whole lives, it is an invitation to remain open and unattached in order to commit oneself to regular volunteer service, career aspirations, family obligations, and stewardship within our faith communities.

Any vocational choice is a response to our fundamental call as Christians to grow more deeply in our love for God and love of others. Our vocation is our path to holiness, it is our response to God's unique call in our lives. We are each called to live our lives as a response to God's love whether we choose to remain single, join together with another in marriage, enter a religious community, or spend our lives serving the poor, teaching children, ministering to the sick, or engaging in professional roles for the betterment of society. We have to ask ourselves, what does God's call to love look like for me?

For many, the single life is a stop on the way to something else. As a single person, how can I best serve God as I wait for the call to marriage or religious life? How am I serving God and loving others through the time I spend traveling, volunteering, dating, pursuing a hobby, or advancing my career?

There are others who are called to be single forever. They are best suited to serve God and love others in a unique way where singlehood is their true vocation. Ask yourself: How does my independence and freedom help me to serve God and love others? Do my lifestyle choices, time commitments, and financial obligations reflect a desire to grow deeper in love with God and others?

Whether we find ourselves single for now or single forever, we should ask, "How am I serving God and loving others at *every* stage of life?" Ultimately, our vocation is to love God with our whole selves and throughout our entire life.

**Choosing Priesthood: What If...::: ***Mark Mossa, S.J.*

I didn't become a priest because I couldn't get a date. I say that not only to affirm my masculinity, but because some people see the priesthood as a "fall back" for the romantically inept. My choice of religious life and priesthood had nothing to do with that. True, I balked at an early opportunity for marriage. And, as I aged into my twenties, family and friends worried whether I would find someone else. But I was not hopeless. There was even someone I got close to as I was trying to figure out the vocation question, someone about whom I still wonder, "What if?"

Recently I was looking at a photo of that same someone, with her husband and children. I felt a twinge of regret—*that could have been me.* It put me in a funk for an afternoon. But a chance to celebrate Mass, help someone through a crisis, and laugh at dinner with my fellow Jesuits soon reminded me of the joys of this life. Though I could be doing something else, living some other way, I'm not sure that I *could* be the "someone else" it would require.

"So, you don't want to get married, have kids?" she asked when I told her of my decision to give the Jesuits a try. "That's not it at all," I remember telling her, my heart aching a bit. "I would love that!" It wasn't about what I wanted—though what God wanted might mean sacrificing the joy that I knew married life would offer me.

Every once in a while it does strike me as strange that I'm a priest, and that I did not get married and start a family. But, mostly, it doesn't. In my ministry to the sick and dying, in teaching my students and in my everyday encounters with others as a Jesuit and a priest, God reveals the wisdom of it. I hardly revel in being single. It's often lonely coming home at night when my housemates are not around, or traveling alone on an airplane full of strangers. Then, I look to Jesus for a reminder of what he once told me in prayer—*I want you to be with me.*

I don't miss the version of the single life in which every social event meant being on the lookout for the woman of my dreams. But I do now have the confidence, which I only had an inkling of in that awkward conversation fifteen years ago. Despite the occasional sadness of not having one intimate lifetime companion and children of my own, I have put myself in the place where, for reasons only God completely knows, I can best make God present in the lives of those to whom I'm given. It's not so much my "singleness" as this single-mindedness about God's purpose that sustains me. That I can be used this way by God still amazes me, and that outshines the "what ifs?" that haunt my duller days.

**Scripture to Remember**

Blessed are those who trust in the Lord, whose trust is the Lord. (Jeremiah 17:7)

Those who find their life will lose it, and those who lose their life for my sake will find it. (Matthew 10:39)

> I do not cease to give thanks for you as I remember you in my prayers. I pray that the God of our Lord Jesus Christ, the Father of glory, may give you a spirit of wisdom and revelation as you come to know him, so that, with the eyes of your heart enlightened, you may know what is the hope to which he has called you, what are the riches of his glorious inheritance among the saints, and what is the immeasurable greatness of his power for us who believe, according to the working of his great power. (Ephesians 1:16–19)

**For Reflection**

1. Is religious life a possibility for me? Why or why not?
2. Where do I fit into God's plan of love? How am I being called to love God and share God's love with others?
3. Who in my life helps me to listen for God's call? Who do I call upon to support, challenge, encourage, and affirm my decisions?

**Try This ...**

- Identify single people that you admire and could consider role models. What qualities do you admire in them and what makes them a role model for you?
- Make a list of all the things you have been putting "on hold" until you get married (buying a house, taking a trip, getting a puppy). Give yourself permission to do those things! And, get started on doing at least one of them!
- Create your own Christmas traditions. Take time to drive through your neighborhood to view the lights. Plan a special holiday party with friends. Donate a gift to a local toy drive, nursing home, or homeless shelter. Decorate cookies with your nieces and nephews.
- Monitor your conversations and how you talk about your life. For example, do you complain that you can't find anyone to date or love? Do you trash talk others who are in a relationship? Do you talk positively about how your life is going? Do you encourage others to follow their hopes and dreams?
- Keep a gratitude journal. At the end of each day, write down three things for which you can give thanks. Start small if you have to ("I am grateful for good health, warm sunshine, and a steady job.")
- Is there someone in your life that needs to be forgiven? Is there an event from your past that you need to let go? Take time to write out, with as much detail as you are able, a list of anyone who has hurt you, an account of what happened, and how it made you feel.
- Write a letter to the person who hurt you (you do not need to send it.) Then, write a letter to yourself in response, as if this other person were responding to you. Imagine this person saying

the things you always wanted to hear. Try to hear their side of the story as you write.

- Make your relationship with God a priority in your life. Spend time with the Scriptures before going to Mass on Sunday. Designate a personal prayer space in your home. Make an annual retreat.
- For those facing important decisions (career change, geographical move, taking the next step in a relationship, entering religious life), here are some practical steps for discernment:
  - Carve out some time to really reflect on the decision at hand. Set aside an afternoon at a local coffee shop, book store, or other favorite spot. Make a list of all possible alternatives, and consider the pros and cons of each. Begin and end this time with prayer.
  - Imagine yourself having made the decision. How does it feel to be in that new place, what emotions arise, and what questions still linger? Is your heart filled with fear, hesitation, contentment, or joy?
  - Ask for input from someone you trust or someone who knows you well. Friends, family, a pastor, or spiritual director are an important sounding board for discernment. Often times, these are the people who can help you see more clearly, especially if your own ability to see clearly is clouded by anxiety or fear.
  - Pray boldly. Ask God for what you need. Listen for God's response. Ask God to make your decision abundantly clear. Ask God, "What do you want me to do?"

SECTION TWO

# Living Single With **Purpose**

*Solitude*
*Stewardship*
*Simplicity*
*Friendship*
*Community*

CHAPTER SEVEN

# Living Single With **Solitude**

*Our language has wisely sensed the two sides of being alone. It has created the word "loneliness" to express the pain of being alone, and the word "solitude" to express the glory of being alone.*—Paul Tillich[1]

## Combating Single Myth # 7: **Being Single Means Being Alone**

One of my favorite chores in the summertime is getting up early each morning to water the flowers outside my condo building. As I stand in awe of the sun shimmering through the trees, I feel a deep sense of connection to our Creator God. In a strange way, I also feel closely connected to my mom, a master gardener, even though she lives five hundred miles away. Furthermore, I am never really alone standing out on the front walk. Early morning runners and dog walkers share a smile or simple hello, and occasionally a neighbor will pause to say thanks for the way our small stretch of greenery brightens up the urban landscape.

I do a lot of things by myself, but I have learned that there is a big difference between being alone and being lonely. We all experience loneliness from time to time in its various forms. Loneliness accompanies everyday disappointments like a bad day at work, a parking ticket, or the stomach flu. In those times when life seems unmanageable, I am keenly aware of my desire for someone to reassure me that life is not so bad. Surely, nothing is more unsettling than the feeling of being alone when surrounded by a crowd of people, an experience not exclusive to singles. Married people experience loneliness, as do those who live within an intentional community. Loneliness happens when those we love have left us or are gone for a specified period of time, like the loneliness we feel when a friend moves or a parent dies. Even more than a physical absence, loneliness indicates an absence of the self from the self. We miss the qualities within ourselves that only another person can bring to light, like their ability to make us laugh or carry on a meaningful conversation.

In a unique way, singles face the question of choosing to attend events (weddings, company holiday parties, family gatherings) alone and risk feeling out of place in a room full of couples. I was once seated at a table full of even-numbered guests and met with awkward stares while everyone tried to figure out who should occupy the one empty seat.

Another time, at a coworker's wedding, as the lone single in the group, I was seated at a table with the photographer, the minister, and the socially awkward cousin. We ask ourselves, "Is it OK to go by myself? If I decide to bring a guest, who do I ask? And how do I make it clear to my date and everyone who sees us together, that we are just friends?"

In the spiritual life the word "solitude" best expresses the contentment one feels when we are at peace with our aloneness. In the busyness of life, most people find that a bit of downtime goes a long way to provide respite for our weary bodies and puts life into perspective. One does not need to escape to the desert for months at a time or spend a year alone in the wilderness to achieve solitude.

Although, it does require us to carve out time and create space to intentionally practice being alone.

In her spiritual memoir, Benedictine sister Joan Chittister shares how she once thought about becoming a hermit, whereupon she discovers that what she truly desires is a regular discipline of solitude in everyday life and not a permanent commitment of solitude for the rest of her life. She describes solitude as "the kind of space that soothes the soul and eventually makes us useful to others again by enabling us to deal with the demons of the day."[2] She goes on to reflect on the spiritual outlook necessary for a solitary life. True solitude requires that we face our personal demons and our past, and when we can no longer run from the true self found in solitude, we open ourselves to God's presence here and now.

Solitude is not only possible but necessary for one to thrive in the single life.

**Only Where the Heart Can Go:::** *Maggi Van Dorn*

We all know them. That friend who always seems to be in a relationship, who is never single for more than a few months and miraculously pulls the next lover from the shadowy side wings of a theatrical breakup—the serial dater. Maybe we are them.

The last time we brushed up against real solitude was around age fourteen. Do you remember the feeling of being in the world as your own person, without reading your worth from the eyes of a boyfriend or girlfriend? Yes, there were oodles of insecurity, but there was also the steady company you kept with yourself before ever knowing what it was like to be bound up with another.

I endlessly exalt in the secret riches of the single life, especially to friends who have not tasted it in years. When one of my best friends,

Jessica, broke off a three-year relationship, I challenged her: "Stay single for a minimum of six months. I dare you. Just try it!"

There is nothing more instructive about single living than an evening alone on the couch with nothing but the sound of the dishwasher gurgling, wondering if your friends secretly conspired to turn off their phones in a cosmic effort to let you feel the utter depths of your single, solitary existence. Yes, the single life is at times lonesome, but it also begs the question: *Aren't we always alone, in or out of a relationship?*

Even in the most intimate of partnerships there are unavoidable differences in temperament, communication, and desire—all of which can be painfully isolating. Heartache is most poignant when we find ourselves missing the person seated right beside us.

For ages, Christian mystics have been testifying to the fulfillment that is found in God alone, while implying how foolish it is for us to seek lasting peace through another person. And yet, many of these sages remain acutely sensitive to the longings of the human heart, including this line inspired by mystic Meister Eckhart, "We weep when light does not reach our hearts. We wither like fields if someone close does not rain their kindness upon us."[3]

We never stop asking to be loved, because we never stop needing it. And yet, no one over age seventeen would publicly admit that they expect their boyfriend or girlfriend to "complete them." It just sounds corny. But my, do we wail when some need or romantic desire of ours goes unmet, no matter how subtle that touch may be!

So what would it mean to know your own hunger and restlessness, to feel it in the pit of your stomach, and to resist the compulsion to feed it right away? What might soothe your longings when another person, friend or lover, isn't meant to? It's a question worth churning over with the rock-a-bye lull of the dishwasher, because ultimately, all of our relationships must draw from an emotional maturity that distinguishes what others can give from what we must find on our own.

Through many of my own solitary nights, I have found it helpful to allow that aching space some breathing room. Instead of agonizing over what is missing, I focus on what is actually present, breathing in gratitude, and releasing the incessant desire for more. When I recline into the richness of the present, my world becomes full again, and I, so capable of giving to it.

It takes time and practice to feel your way toward peace, to memorize the inner path to your deepest center. And the truth is, I would never think of sitting still with my desires if I didn't have to or if I lived under the illusion that another person could possibly satisfy them. Staying single for a time means staying with your desires long enough to know when they are reasonable and when they are insatiable. It is a necessary interruption for anyone enslaved to the pattern of jumping from one relationship to the next and expecting the impossible from them. From what I can see, a heart at peace with itself is a blessing upon every human relationship.

**Spiritual Principle: Solitude**

What would happen if you would sit down and pay attention to the quiet or allow yourself to spend time alone? We live in a noisy world filled with constant chatter via our iPods, cable television, social networking websites, and the endless advertising that fills our peripheral vision. We've become so accustomed to external stimuli that silence feels awkward, and there is the subtle temptation to rush to fill that space with something else, be it music, television, food, shopping, the Internet, video games, or exercise. Our response to silence is to make it go away in order to escape the insatiable feeling that we might suddenly self-destruct from being by ourselves.

The practice of solitude takes time and practice, and true solitude involves more than being by yourself. Living alone does not guarantee solitude, just as living with other people does not constitute community. All of us will experience some degree of loneliness before ever reaching true solitude. (Perhaps you will consider some of the exercises from the "Try This" sections throughout the book for ideas!)

Solitude extends the invitation to accept myself for who I am, celebrates what I have accomplished, and acknowledges the dreams that have gone unfinished thus far in my life. At the same time, solitude also reveals our inadequacies, my weakness, our failures, and my own sinfulness.

In the silence, when all else is stripped away, we are left alone with our whole selves. The blessedness and the woundedness of our souls are there to behold in their fullness. In solitude, God meets us where we are which is often in the messiness and brokenness of life. When we allow God to reveal these things to us, only then can God heal us and bring us the peace we truly desire.

Jesus himself provides a wonderful example of prayer and solitude. In the Gospels, we often hear about Jesus going off to a quiet place to pray. Perhaps the most significant account of prayer is detailed in the forty days Jesus spends in the wilderness (Matthew 4:1–11). At the very outset of his public ministry, Jesus was drawn into the desert by the Holy Spirit. It is there, alone in the wilderness, that even Jesus could not escape the darkness of solitude.

Jesus, like us in all things but sin, is tempted by the devil three times. Here he comes face to face with some fundamental human temptations including pride, fame, power, control, and self-importance. Jesus was tempted in ways that were indicative of the temptations he was likely to face as a teacher, preacher, and healer.

While he comes to an acute awareness of his temptations, he never gives in to them.

Furthermore, Jesus leaves the desert with a keen awareness of his mission and purpose in life, prepared to enter into the demands of public ministry. One of the joys of solitude is that it opens us to discover our true calling and place in life. Spiritual writer Henri Nouwen reminds us:

> Solitude is the place where we find our identity. It is the place where we take a few moments in quiet before God to see who we are in relationship to God and to each other. In solitude we listen and wait to "hear" the voice of the One who loves us and who calls us to deeper love.
>
> Solitude is the place where we are with God and God alone, and where we can come to understand our own most individual call.[4]

Solitude, especially a regular discipline of solitude, exposes us to the mystery of God's divine goodness. The glory of being alone is coming face to face with ourselves, seeing our beauty and our pain, and becoming aware of God's great love for each of us in the midst of it all. Solitude is the place where we discover that our self worth is not defined by our single status.

**Scripture to Remember**

And after he had dismissed the crowds, he went up the mountain by himself to pray. When evening came, he was there alone.... (Matthew 14:23)

Where can I go from your spirit?
Or where can I flee from your presence? (Psalm 139:7)

> He said, "Go out and stand on the mountain before the Lord, for the Lord is about to pass by." Now there was a great wind, so strong that it was splitting mountains and breaking rocks in pieces before the Lord, but the Lord was not in the wind; and after the wind an earthquake, but the Lord was not in the earthquake; and after the earthquake a fire, but the Lord was not in the fire; and after the fire a sound of sheer silence. When Elijah heard it, he wrapped his face in his mantle and went out and stood at the entrance of the cave. Then there came a voice to him that said, "What are you doing here, Elijah?" (1 Kings 19:11–13)

**For Reflection**

1. How do I respond in moments of loneliness? Do I intentionally try to avoid it or fill the emptiness with material things?
2. Consider the difference between being alone, feeling lonely, and achieving solitude. How do aloneness, loneliness, and solitude come into play in my single life?
3. What has been my experience of solitude? What is one practice that I can incorporate into my life to bring about a greater sense of solitude?

CHAPTER EIGHT

# Living Single With **Stewardship**

*The size of one's home should never dictate the outreach of one's heart.* —Luci Swindoll[1]

## Combating Single Myth #8: **Being Single is a Selfish Way to Live**

Perhaps the greatest misperception or myth about the single life is that singles have endless amounts of time and a lot of extra cash on hand, and we're selfish about how we spend it. Sure, there are single people who don't think twice when spending money on a luxurious vacation, classy furniture, or an expensive night out on the town. We all know people who are fixated on keeping up appearances, buying the latest electronic gadgets, sporting designer labels, or spending a day at the spa.

None of these are bad things as long as we indulge in moderation. Life's little luxuries become problematic, however, when we care more about our material goods than we do about people. It may be time to reassess our spending habits if our "stuff" gets in the way of our relationships with others, causes us to lose sight of the needs of the poor, or impacts our relationship with God.

There are always exceptions to the classic stereotype. I know many singles, including myself, who take joy in lavishing gifts upon our nieces and nephews. A friend once commented how her youngest son loves having Uncle Bob, who is not married, as his godfather because he gives the best presents! One of my greatest joys is having the financial means to drop a check into the lap of my favorite charity at Christmas.

At the other extreme, we can certainly find a few singles who selfishly save money. They are so frugal with their funds that they cannot imagine giving to charity, buy only the bare necessities, rarely dine out, wouldn't imagine ever taking a vacation, and see those who spend money on golf outings and expensive cars as wasteful. If someone is saving money for a rainy day, I sometimes wonder if he or she will actually have the heart to spend it when that day comes.

Singles face the "selfish" stereotype not only in regard to money, but also when it comes to sharing our time and energy, especially regarding familial obligations and a single person's role in making family decisions. I have a friend who worries about his autistic younger brother and his parents' ability to provide for him as they age. Another single friend has gone out of his way to be involved in the lives of his nieces and nephews after the death of his sister. And many families inevitably face the question of how to best care for aging parents.

Some single people are in an advantageous position to respond to any variety of family emergencies. On the other hand, I've met singles who are not given a choice, or who feel obligated to step into such a role, when married siblings insist that they have already done their share by raising their own children. By not taking on the added responsibility, the single person is labeled "selfish" without his or her unique circumstances being considered, as with others involved. Other times, the single sibling is not consulted at all, or they find that their married siblings' opinions carry more weight in family matters.

Some singles are frugal, some spend money like it's going out of style, some are deep in debt, and some give generously to charity because they have the financial means. We could find people who fit any one of these stereotypes regardless of their relationship status. Not all single people live like Daddy Warbucks; not every unmarried person acts like Ebeneezer Scrooge. However, being single does provide some unique opportunities and challenges when it comes to setting financial priorities.

**Seek First the Kingdom:::**

*Christine Harrell*

It's funny when people assume that singles live selfish, indulgent, Epicurean lives. We blow money on luxuries such as lavish vacations, spa treatments, fancy cars, expensive drinks, memberships at yuppie gyms and condo lofts. We don't give to charity and we date tons of people.

Yes, my life is fraught with material luxuries! I take vacations, but when I get to my destination I stay in a hostel, just four stars away from a five-star hotel! I get a massage twice a year, but only if I have a discount coupon. I get a pedicure at the nail shop in Chinatown once a year. I finally bought a car: a used, four-door coupe that gets me where I need to go. Sometimes I eat out with friends, and I buy one drink (maybe) as well as blow a whopping ten dollars on my meal. I work out at home with my two exercise DVDs. I even have my own place in a very un-hip part of town surrounded by factories—but hey, no roommates!

That's glamorous, right? I suppose I am a bit of a Scrooge: I've only donated money to Lupus research, animal shelters, Vincentian priests and nuns, as well as natural disaster relief. I also volunteered once a month all over the city before the volunteer group folded. I guess I should have found somewhere else to volunteer once that group ended—selfish me! Oh, I give to church too, but you're supposed to do that.

If single people are selfish and indulgent, I must be an outlier. My Catholic upbringing ingrained in me the idea of living simply and giving to the poor. In fact, in Luke 21:1–4, Jesus praises the widow who gave all she had to the collection plate rather than ones who gave out of their surplus. I was taught and believe that all the money and material possessions of the world mean nothing if you don't have the love of God. I try to listen and live by this quote attributed to St. Elizabeth Ann Seton: "Live simply so that others may simply live."

True joy and fulfillment come from living the life God calls us to live. Perhaps that life for me is perpetual singlehood, but that's OK. We are supposed to store up treasures in heaven, not on earth. If this is the life God has in store for me, I have faith that it will be perfect, even if it's lacking in some material comforts.

I do, however, want to move away from the factories.

## Spiritual Principle: Stewardship

> *From everyone to whom much has been given, much will be required; and from the one to whom much has been entrusted, even more will be demanded.* (Luke 12:48)

Because most single people support only themselves, many of us are endowed with more financial means or discretionary income. (However, some would argue that singles are at a financial disadvantage because we do not share living expenses such as rent or mortgage, telephone, cable, utilities, and so on, with a partner.) Furthermore, singles often have more flexibility and freedom with which to use our time. It becomes all the more necessary then that singles carefully discern how to best spend our money, devote our time, and bestow our talents.

Several years ago, I found myself at a crossroads in terms of financial priorities. Until that time, I spent most of my single years with few financial worries. Armed with a new job, a freshly minted master's degree and, for the first time, my own home, I was confronted with shifting financial priorities. Around this time, I stumbled upon a magazine interview with Melinda Gates, wife of Microsoft founder Bill Gates, where she talked about the Bill and Melinda Gates Foundation and laid out the foundation's mission and her personal philosophy of giving.

One would think that with billions of dollars the Gates Foundation could give endless amounts of money to any and all organizations. Because they have so much to give, they give very intentionally, consciously giving large sums of money to causes that have a long-term impact on a global scale, with the potential to benefit the greatest number of people. Two questions drive the Gates's decision to give to an organization, "Which problems affect the most people? And which have been neglected in the past?"[2]

My capacity for giving will never reach the level of the Gates Foundation, but I am now asking myself, "What are the questions, issues, and causes that drive my desire to give? What motivates me to give to some charities and not to others? With whom do I share my financial resources, and to whom do I give my dedication of time? How much can I afford to give? And where does my giving have the greatest impact?"

As Catholics and Christians, we are all called to responsible stewardship. Stewardship is more than giving a certain percentage of our income to the church. It is a spiritual task and a way of life in which we recognize our responsibility to be accountable for and share our gifts with one another. All that we have is a gift from God. Stewardship encompasses the multitude of ways in which we dedicate our time, share our skills, and contribute financial resources to those in need. Stewardship is about thoughtfully giving back as a way of saying thanks for all that has been given to us.

If you were to track your spending for an entire month, how would you feel about where your money goes? Consider how you spend money and how you feel about the financial choices you make. The Gospel of Matthew says, "Where your treasure is, there your heart will be also" (6:19). Where is your heart in regard to your treasure?

Whether your treasure pays for medical expenses, buys groceries, invests in the stock market, or gives to charity, ultimately your heart goes with it. The spiritual challenge is to keep our hearts focused on God. Good stewardship, prayerfully discerning where and how much to give, should result in the disposition of our hearts leaning closer toward God.

Much of the issue around money has to do with our need for control, and money is often equated to self-worth. In our American culture, a person is deemed "successful" by the size of their house, car, or bank account. The fear of not having enough money threatens our sense of security and control over our livelihoods. Some people worry about putting food on the table or taking care of immediate needs like health insurance or transportation. Others of us worry about our ability to maintain a certain standard of living, how we are perceived by our peers, and perhaps most significantly, how we see ourselves.

At the heart of stewardship is a fundamental trust that God will provide everything that we need. There will be enough, even when we give away what we cherish or make a conscious effort to live with less. Everything we have is God's gift to us. Ultimately, stewardship is a way to express our thanks by joyfully sharing with others what we have received from God.

**Scripture to Remember**

Each of you must give as you have made up your mind, not reluctantly or under compulsion, for God loves a cheerful giver. And God is able to provide you with every blessing in abundance, so that by always having enough of everything, you may share abundantly in every good work. (2 Corinthians 9:7–8)

Whoever is faithful in a very little is faithful also in much; and whoever is dishonest in a very little is dishonest also in much. No slave can serve two masters; for a slave will either hate the one and love the other, or be devoted to the one and despise the other. You cannot serve God and wealth. (Luke 16:10, 13)

I know what it is to have little, and I know what it is to have plenty. In any and all circumstances I have learned the secret of being well fed and of going hungry, of having plenty and of being in need. I can do all things through him who strengthens me. (Philippians 4:12–13)

**For Reflection**

1. Where do I place my trust when it comes to issues of money and financial security? Do I trust that God will provide everything I need?
2. Where is my heart in regard to my treasure? How do I feel about where I spend my money? Do my spending choices draw me closer to God or away from God?
3. Do I willingly share my time, talents, financial resources with others in joy and gratitude? Does my spending adequately reflect a care for the poor and the least among us?

CHAPTER NINE

# Living Single With **Simplicity**

*It seems to me that whatever our work, we need to build into it ways of reminding ourselves that there are self-imposed limits to what we need or want or are capable of. We have to determine what those limits are and stick to them if we are to be in touch with God, who is always "enough."* –Greg Pierce[1]

## Combating Single Myth #9: **Singles Tend to Define Themselves by Their Work**

"By 9:00 AM the morning is half over!" To this day, my dad sticks by this philosophy and the oft-repeated mantra I heard growing up, "There is no such thing as sleeping in!"

From a very early age, I was destined to become a perfectionist and an overachiever. I got good grades, worked hard, and was determined to succeed at whatever I tried. Failure was never an option. So, it is no surprise that the temptation to define myself by what I do for a living is one that I struggle with and rally against more than any other myth. The assumption that "since you don't have a family, you can spend more time at work" is not only a false one, but it is also a considerable temptation for those of us who are without a partner or children at home.

In talking with friends and colleagues, I have often found that single people face a certain social inequality defined by the added pressure to do more and have more. Colleagues expect that you have more time and energy to spend on work-related priorities. When someone needs to stay late to finish a project or wait for a client call, the single person becomes the natural first choice. Furthermore, especially early in their careers, single people work hard to get ahead and make a place for themselves in their chosen field. We are faced with expectations from colleagues, added pressure to impress the boss, and the extra demands we place on ourselves. Having an endless amount of time and energy may give us the motivation we need to keep ourselves moving along the fast track, but it also puts single people at greater risk of getting burned out or being taken advantage of.

Singles also contend with the stereotype that we cannot be trusted. Perhaps there is that one single guy or girl in the office who has been known to throw back a few too many drinks at happy hour only to stagger into the office late the next morning. In another work-related incident, a friend of mine tells a story where she was told by their HR manager, "Whatever you do, don't hire another twenty-five year old who is just going to run off and get married after a year!" Some companies are better than others about hiring women, hiring young people, offering internships, agreeing to flex time, and providing necessary benefits. Yet, some singles are faced with situations where employers question their dedication, and there is a myth that single people (especially those who are young and single) can be irresponsible.

Regardless of age, experience, education, and line of work, singles find themselves pulled in multiple directions trying to balance work, social life, family obligations, and volunteer commitments as well as managing our own physical, emotional, and spiritual well-being.

**Finding the Balance:::** *Clarissa Aljentera*

Balancing a new career with one's life can be precarious, and it was never something that I managed well. It was so easy to succumb to the nagging work cell phone. It was so easy to rewrite a few more sentences that always led to a few more paragraphs. It was a never-ending grind. And I fell in love with it at an early age.

Balancing work and life was a concept I wanted to integrate into my life, but I did not know where to begin. Do I begin with saying "no" when my editors asked for an extra story or an extra hour? Do I ignore my inner voice that wants to scale the journalistic ladder? Do I quit striving to be the go-to person in the company?

Early on, I made it clear to family and friends that my career, my first love, always had to come first. That was my first—and biggest—mistake I made as a young professional: erecting a gigantic wall around me that made it impossible to climb over and to meet people, and impossible for people to enter my barricaded fortress. This was not healthy.

Instead of tending to relationships and friendships, I kept telling myself that finishing a degree in journalism meant that I was dedicated to the field until the bitter end. "Tired, worn out, stressed" became the words that I and other folks around me championed because it meant we were getting somewhere in our careers.

Those words multiplied in my head dozens of times. My mantra was consistently, "One more day." Finally, I cracked. Or rather, my work life shattered me. I finally had it with trying to fit myself into a mold of work that was clearly unhealthy and that cultivated an existence where loving myself came last and pleasing others came first. My overburdened journalist lifestyle had slowly pushed me to my second career in ministry.

I always believed that I could take care of myself as a single, working professional. But I was not really caring for my needs of *community*—a fine line for many young professionals.

Through the mess of my career, I still managed to attend Mass every week, not knowing what I was looking for exactly, but knowing that something about gathering with a community of believers comforted me. Soon, like many people in their mid-twenties, I began reexamining my faith life more. I became open to finding a community of young professionals who wanted to talk about faith in their lives.

It took many sleepless nights and many nights when I cried myself to sleep to see that I was not caring for myself in a way that a young professional should. I did not cry tears of loneliness from not being in a relationship, but tears of frustration that I had to walk away from my work.

I had to take better care of myself, not because someone was telling me to change my life, but because I needed to be more attentive to *my* needs. I forced myself to take classes at the community college in psychology, theater, and Spanish to fill a love of learning. I volunteered with the Boys and Girls Club at lunchtime to read to a first-grader every week. I took time by myself to watch a California sunset while perching on my favorite rock overlooking Big Sur.

Balancing both work and life continues to be a struggle. But the true test of living out the vocation of the single life is that I am called to be in community and relationship as much as my friends who are married. The test for me begins every morning when I step into the world knowing that an extra hour at work would not hurt anyone. But it's a vicious cycle to step away from. Living more intentionally in a greater community takes more attention and prayer in my own life so that I can be a more loving person to myself and those around me.

**Spiritual Principle: Simplicity**

A friend once suggested that if you want to be respected as a single person you need to be a hero or a martyr. She cited her favorite role models for single living, such as Jean Donovan, Peggy Roach, Dorothy Day, and others known for their radical commitment to the gospel and dedication to the poor.

At times, singles live with this false notion that we can and should do it all. Those who try to undertake every social obligation, workplace demand, and volunteer commitment soon discover that life gets complicated. It is easy to lose focus, and the more we try to do everything, the more difficult it becomes to do any one thing really well. The everyday saints admired by my friend were not heroes because they did everything. Rather, they knew the work to which God called them and they made that work the focus of their lives.

Simplicity, as a spiritual practice, is about knowing what is important and what is not. Simplicity does not mean that you have to adhere to a boring or bland lifestyle when it comes to clothing, home décor, or personal preferences. Nor does it require that you decrease your social obligations or have less fun. It is about gaining freedom from unnecessary chaos and overcoming predictable obstacles.

Sure, there is chaos imposed upon us that is often beyond our control, like natural disasters or a sudden illness. Some workplaces have regular peak times, like the beginning of the school year for teachers or the April 15 tax deadline for accountants. There will always be family emergencies and times when we need to go out of our way to make ourselves available to friends, family, and community members.

But then, there is the self-imposed chaos that results when we are not able to set healthy boundaries between our work and personal life, when our priorities fall out of line, when we allow ourselves to be swayed by other people's demands, or when we give in to the temptation to define our lives by our career goals or personal achievements.

Robert Wicks, a leading author on the intersection of spirituality and psychology, says,

> "Simplicity" allows us to be free to both enjoy and let go of all of life because we know there is more; we trust that God will provide us with what we need at each successive stage of life—even after we die. An attitude like this allows us to be concerned about our family and friends, but not pulled down by them. An attitude of simplicity encourages us to enjoy all we have, but not become addicted to people or things so we feel permanently lost without them.[2]

One exercise in simplicity and setting priorities is to ask at the beginning of each day, "What does God need most from me?" Maintaining a healthy balance sometimes means saying "yes" when you think you should say "no" and saying "no" when you think you should say "yes." Some people have the propensity to say "yes" to everything. If that is you, consider: When was the last time you said "no"? When was the last time you set limits on someone else's control over your time? Furthermore, when was the last time you said "yes" to some good, healthy fun?

There are times when God needs us to take care of ourselves first in order that we might better care for others. I think of this like the warning emphasized during airplane flight safety instructions: "In case of an emergency, put on your own oxygen mask first before assisting others." Our ability to first care for ourselves prepares us to tend to the needs of others. Likewise, our ability to turn down an invitation or step away from a situation may be someone else's opportunity to share their gifts.

Setting priorities is not a selfish move; it is good self-care. We live such busy lives that we worry about wasting time if we're not doing something productive. Doing things which fill our souls allows us to be more attentive to our relationships and to recognize God's action in our lives. This includes activities like setting time aside for prayer, going for a run through a forest preserve, scheduling a regular night out with friends, taking a vacation, attending a weekend retreat, playing golf, or whatever else brings joy.

When we give in to the temptation to do it all, we end up acquiring responsibilities and emotional baggage that we don't necessarily want or need. As we simplify our lives, focusing on those things that are most important and most meaningful, we should discover that our day-to-day lives feel a bit lighter and easier, even on those days when we are expected to work long hours. And too, we are more prepared to face the necessary demands of work, family emergencies, unexpected home repairs, or other crisis situations.

**Scripture to Remember**

For thus said the LORD GOD, the Holy One of Israel:
In returning and rest you shall be saved;
in quietness and in trust shall be your strength. (Isaiah 30:15)

Come to me, all you that are weary and are carrying heavy burdens, and I will give you rest. Take my yoke upon you, and learn from me; for I am gentle and humble in heart, and you will find rest for your souls. For my yoke is easy, and my burden is light. (Matthew 11:28–30)

[B]ut those who wait for the LORD shall renew their strength,
they shall mount up with wings like eagles,

they shall run and not be weary,
they shall walk and not faint. (Isaiah 40:31)

**For Reflection**

1. Where does work fall in comparison to other priorities in my life? Do I give in to the temptation to define my life by my career?
2. What are the things I do for fun and recreation? How do I find balance and practice good self-care?
3. What activities take up the greatest amount of my time or emotional energy? Are there areas of my life that could be simplified?

CHAPTER TEN

# Living Single With **Friendship**

*And let your best be for your friend.*
*If he must know the ebb of your tide,*
*let him know its flood also.*
*For what is your friend that you should*
*seek him with hours to kill?*
*Seek him always with hours to live.*—Khalil Gibran[1]

## Combating Single Myth #10: **Men and Women Can't Be Just Friends**

Ed and I met several years ago on a young adult retreat and discovered we have some mutual friends. We live in the same neighborhood and routinely visit the same local coffee shop. Preparing to write this book, I asked Ed if he'd like to grab coffee and give me a guy's perspective. We had a great conversation, and he brought up some interesting points I hadn't considered, some of which made their way into this chapter!

However, I often wonder what people think when they see a guy and a girl together at the coffee shop. If I mention to someone that I went out for coffee with Abby or Kelli or Meredith, it usually goes by without much notice. But the second I mention, "I had coffee with Ed," or, "I ran into Mike at the grocery store," or, "I got a call from Jim last night," then the barrage of questions begins: Who is this? How long have you known him? Where is he from? How did you meet? Are you interested in him? Is he cute?

When it comes to our acquaintances with people of the opposite sex, inquiring minds always want to know if there is something "more" to our friendship. Perhaps this stems from a cultural expectation to be married or our personal dreams to one day find a life partner. Can men and women be friends just for the sake of friendship? Or do we always think about male-female relationships solely in terms of dating? Do you find yourself basing relationships with the other gender strictly in terms of their potential to become a romantic partner? Or are there other qualities that motivate you to seek and maintain their friendship?

I'd like to suggest that men and women can indeed be friends, without the added pressure of something more to their relationship. Sure, there may be the occasional awkward tension or the charged energy of romantic interest. But there is value in getting to know this other person even without any physical attraction. It is possible to be friends and not fall in love.

**Just Friends:::** *Katie Kustusch*

"No, he is not my husband," I replied to the elderly woman staring at me quizzically. I was almost too surprised to even say that! In her mind, if I was with a "nice young man" visiting her in the nursing home where she lived, of course, we would be married to each other. No matter that this "nice young man" and I were both happily single and just happened to be placed together on the same team on our service trip.

Perhaps I wouldn't have chosen this topic for my reflection if this was an isolated event. I am smiling as I write this, knowing that if you've been single for any amount of time, a similar situation has probably happened to you. Maybe it was at the store or a friend's party, maybe it was your great aunt who said something! Wherever it was, after getting over the surprise of it, you probably realized just how much you value the friendships you have with guys. I have been blessed to have several really good friends who happen to be men. Some are married, some are single, and each is a gift to me. St. Paul had it right when he said (I paraphrase): "In Christ, there is no division of free person or slave, male or female." In Christ, I am offered the gift of friendship with all kinds of people, some of whom I might not be friends with had we not met through our common Christian community.

Free to be myself and to set good boundaries, I have found such wonderful blessings, as a single woman, in my friendships with my guy friends. Whoever said that if we aren't married or dating at the moment, then we aren't allowed to have friends of the opposite sex? Of course, it comes with extra work. If I want to stay friends with some men, I choose to stay friends with their wives or girlfriends. Likewise, if one of my female friends starts dating someone, her significant other naturally becomes a part of our circle of friends. I choose to be a third wheel a lot, but the way I figure it, I get two friends instead of one out of the deal! Furthermore, if I am friends with a single guy, it means that I don't abuse our friendship by pretending we're dating if we're really not.

Sometimes though, it really helps to have the perspective of the opposite gender. Often, I find myself becoming a better woman because I've learned something only a man could teach me. It's refreshing to have the honest, unvarnished truth from good friends, whether men or women. We help each other to grow more fully into the men and women God is calling us to be when we have someone from the opposite sex help us learn what it means to be a man or a woman of God.

The main way that I've met most of my good guy friends has been through ministry. I volunteer with my church, a local nonprofit, and a retreat program for teens. People assume a lot about those who should or could be called as coworkers in the vineyard. It has been my joy and privilege, and sometimes immensely frustrating, to dispel those assumptions. So, no, he is not my husband, but yes, we are here, as friends and brothers and sisters in Christ.

**Spiritual Principle: Friendship**

Friendships are essential to the single life. Friends often fill the need for intimacy in our lives. We seek someone who shares our passions and intellectual pursuits, someone who will share our joy and understand our frustrations, someone to whom we can reveal the privileged details of our lives, someone to have fun with and share common interests, and a person with whom we can be our true selves. Few know us this closely.

Strong friendships are built over time and take work from both sides. Friendship requires reciprocal commitment, a sense of give-and-take, and the ability to meet one another at the same level. Nothing is worse than the so-called "friend" who doesn't return calls or the lopsided friendship in which one person always initiates and the other simply follows.

Friendship also requires authentic sharing and mutual vulnerability. If a friendship is going to bring us to the level of "being known" that we desire, it requires self-knowledge and self-revelation. I need to be honest and allow myself to be vulnerable in front of the other. A friend is one to whom I can speak the truth about myself, how I see the world, and what I observe in others.

In return, our friends know and accept us for who we are, see us at our best and worst, and love us anyway. Friendship provides a mirror of self-awareness by showing us our strengths and helping us to name our weaknesses. A friend is one who always has the best interest of the other in mind.

Perhaps the greatest challenge of friendship is that friends are not always permanent. There is no public commitment ceremony, and we don't take vows in friendship. Like all good relationships, friendship requires fidelity, mutual trust, and forgiveness. Friends are our answer to the question, "Who cares? Who cares *about* me? And who will care *for* me when the time comes?"

We may never say it aloud, but we expect our friends to be true to us "in good times and in bad, in sickness and in health." Inevitably, the longer we are friends, the better chance there is that we will one day realize the other person is not perfect (and neither are we), they disappoint us, or we disagree. Forgiveness is essential to friendship, as is our ability to overlook flaws and find goodness in the other.

It is important to choose friends wisely, know your expectations, and not feign affection. Revisiting the criteria for friendship (even in your mind), makes it is easier to stay consistent and committed to your own personal boundaries.

Can men and women be "just friends"? We are predisposed to think of ourselves as separate and unique, but how would you describe those qualities that differentiate the sexes? The biological traits and genetic differences are obvious, but many of our traditional attitudes about men and women are influenced by culture, environment, and our individual upbringing.

Men are expected to be fearless, physically strong, financial providers. Women are affirmed in their roles as caring, nurturing, compassionate homemakers. Yet, our strengths as men and women do not always fall within these categories. My friend Steve, a social worker, has taught me about compassion for the homeless. Jenéne, who owns a complete set of power tools, once spent an afternoon with me installing shelves in my closet. Robert is the best cook among our circle of friends. Kathy, a seasoned corporate executive, guided me through a complex transition with confidence and determination.

God designed men and women as separate beings, but also to be mutually dependent on one another. Franciscan priest Richard Rohr, in describing masculine spirituality, talks about the imbalance that results when men are expected to be the dominant gender and the resulting oppression experienced by women. Simply "reversing roles" does not correct the situation, as some women have learned to manipulate and control others in order to compensate for their perceived "weakness" among their male counterparts. In *From Wild Man to Wise Man: Reflections on Male Spirituality,* Rohr writes: "The liberating gospel of Jesus is that salvation is found not in domination but in partnership, not in power-wielding but in power-sharing.... The spiritually whole person integrates within himself or herself both the masculine and the feminine dimensions of the human spirit."[2]

In the creation story we hear how God created humankind in his own image, "male and female he created them" (Genesis 1:27). To fully know God, we must embrace the unique qualities of both our male and female friends. Our lives are incomplete without the other. As single people we need friends, men and women, with varying skills and interests, who can provide intellectual challenge, spiritual guidance, career advice, and a helping hand when we need it.

More than any other relationship, single people need their friends. They are our source of intimacy, connection, laughter, and fun. Friendship is a place where we are supported and challenged to grow. The twelfth-century Cistercian monk Aelred of Rievaulx offers this timeless reflection on spiritual friendship:

> Your friend is the companion of your soul, to whose spirit you join and attach yours, and so associate yourself that you wish to become one instead of two, since he is one to whom you entrust yourself as to another self, from whom you hide nothing, from whom you fear nothing.[3]

May each of us be blessed to find such a friend!

**Scripture to Remember**

Pleasant speech multiplies friends,
  and a gracious tongue multiplies courtesies.
Let those who are friendly with you be many,
  but let your advisers be one in a thousand.
Faithful friends are a sturdy shelter:
  whoever finds one has found a treasure.
Faithful friends are beyond price;
  no amount can balance their worth. (Sirach 6:5–6, 14–15)

Two are better than one, because they have a good reward for their toil. For if they fall, one will lift up the other; but woe to one who is alone and falls and does not have another to help. (Ecclesiastes 4:9–10)

This is my commandment, that you love one another as I have loved you. No one has greater love than this, to lay down one's life for one's friends. You are my friends if you do what I command you. I do not call you servants any longer, because the servant does not know what the master is doing; but I have called you friends, because I have made known to you everything that I have heard from my Father. (John 15:12–15)

**For Reflection**

1. When thinking about close friends, ask: What is the story of our friendship? How did we first become friends? What are my favorite memories? What struggles have we faced? What sustains our relationship even now?
2. How would I describe the similarities and differences in my friendships with married people, single people, guy friends, and girl friends? What are the different qualities that each bring to our friendship because of unique circumstances and life experience?
3. How important is it that my friends share similar religious beliefs and values? How has faith played a role in my friendships? In what ways do I share my faith with my friends?

## CHAPTER ELEVEN

# Living Single With **Community**

*Each of us is called to answer God's love with her or his life. How can I best respond to God's love? How can I best spread God's love in my life and in others' lives? How can I best lead a loving life? How can I best live out my baptismal call to service? These are key questions.* —Eileen E. O'Brien[1]

## Combating Single Myth #11: **The Church Cares Only About Couples and Families**

Early in my young adult years, I was blessed to find a faith community filled with married and single people of all ages and stages in life. I made great friends, we supported one another in our faith, and together we discerned the choices to which God had called each one of us. Over the years, this church community grew, their needs shifted, and parishioners responded with great generosity. With the support of a talented parish staff, the community established a flourishing social justice ministry, a thriving retreat program, multiple opportunities for adult faith formation, and expanded the adjoining Catholic school and religious education programs. It is a place where I always feel welcome and at home.

Unfortunately, my experience is not shared by all single people. I have met many singles who feel lost or forgotten by their faith community. Some are in parishes where the average person in the pew is the same age as our parents or grandparents, and young singles in particular find it difficult to relate to them. Others are in parishes that support a Catholic school, and the life of the parish primarily revolves around ministry to married couples and families with young children. In this case singles may be invited to babysit during Mass, teach religious education, or assist with the youth group. While some singles are called to share in these ministries, when they are presented as the only options, the community fails to recognize the unique gifts of each individual. Likewise, those who work for the church sometimes mistake "singles ministry" as spiritual and social opportunities for singles to meet one another. While matchmaking is one potential outcome, single people have a lot to offer and share with the church regardless of their relationship status.

We are all called to holiness, regardless of our vocational call, past history, or present relationship status. The documents of Vatican II specifically mention that singles "can also greatly contribute to the holiness and activity of the church." All Christians—single, married, ordained, and vowed religious—are reminded that we grow in holiness by responding to God's call, and we reveal God's love to the world through the unique "conditions, duties, and circumstances of our lives."[2] The church is a place for us to belong, and singles have a unique role to play in the life of the community. It is where we continue to grow in holiness by following the example of Jesus, freely and fully giving ourselves in service to others.

**One in Faith:::** *Bekah Stolhandske McNeel*

When I first encountered my current faith community, it was overrun with toddlers and young married people. The service sounded like an aviary with its squeals and chatter. At first I was as miserable as I expected to be as a single girl, fresh out of graduate school and pretty much friendless in my own hometown. I left most fellowship events with a gnawing awareness of my singlehood, wondering what was wrong with me.

As I grew to love my church in spite of my jealousy and occasional bitterness, I found myself wanting very much to serve and engage it with my whole heart. There were two main obstacles to this task: I viewed everything as a trade-off, and I thought singleness meant saying "yes" to everything.

Everything is a trade-off. Filling up my social calendar was fun, but I saw it as a way to compensate for the quiet nights at home that I was not spending with a special guy. Even more problematic were the hard times. What was the trade-off then? Funerals, doctor's appointments, and minor home disasters were hardly a fair way for God to repay me for his withholding a partner! I thought that God owed me some sort of karmic balance of good and bad. And it seemed that anything God gave me was less than what was best for me. As long as I continued to see my singleness as a bad thing, dealt by a withholding God, I kept looking to the rest of the world to compensate. Community was no different. I started to look to my church to make the loneliness go away and to make up for God's withholding a partner from me.

Singleness means saying "yes" to everything. As I got more involved, I realized that singleness meant that I could say yes to all sorts of things. I could babysit for desperate mothers, go on trips with the college ministry, and spend my weekends volunteering. I could say yes to everything! And, my logical conclusion was that if I *could* say yes, I *should* say yes. That seemed to validate my singleness. But my error here was in the purpose of service. Service is not something we engage in to validate our existence, marital status, income, or anything else. Service is an act of gratitude. The conclusion of this erroneous view of the world culminated in my view of God as a backroom hideout revolutionary leader sending his nameless sycophants out to their death. He didn't care, as long as his cause marched on. I was devoted to the cause—his kingdom and its people—but I resented the Leader.

My view of singleness changed only as my theology changed and Romans 8 revealed so much to me in this regard. Romans says, "He who did not withhold his own Son, but gave him up for all of us, will he not with him also give us everything else?" (8:32). God wants to give us everything we need. Could it be that singleness was God's act of love toward me? Not to make me more productive, not to use me up and then cast me aside, but to bless me and nurture me. It was a lonely state, filled with longing and groaning, but Romans again says, "Likewise the Spirit helps us in our weakness; for we do not know how to pray as we ought, but that very Spirit intercedes with sighs too deep for words" (8:26). God was close to me, feeling that loneliness, and answering to it with sympathy and kindness. He was keeping me single, and that too was an act of kindness. This was not a blow for which to be compensated and not a ploy to keep me laboring along. It was a mysterious love and protection.

As community deepened around me, I found myself sharing excitement, sadness, responsibilities, and help. I learned to be flexible and to make room for people in my schedule. I learned to choose not to be offended and to seek restoration. All of this was from living not in a "special relationship" but in community. Occasionally my discontentment would rage against all of this goodness to say, "But it's not what I want! It's just a substitute." The Spirit responded by speaking to my heart, "It's what you need. It's what is best. And I know it hurts right now, but you can endure it because it's good. It is good!"

In the course of this I realized what the Bible means when it says that it was not good for Adam to be alone. Eve was not God's answer to a romantic longing, as she is so often portrayed to be. Eve was Adam's community. She was his helper, friend, ally, partner, and his "other." Marriage is irreplaceable, yes. But it is not the only way that God provides Eve (community) for Adam (the single person). Community and singleness isn't about making up for the lack. It's about accepting goodness from God for what it is.

**Spiritual Principle: Community**

In her article "Singleness and Spirituality," Francine Cardman asks:

> In relation to single persons, it would be beneficial if we started asking, in a non-exploitative way, not what ministry to singles is, but what the ministry of singles is. What gifts do they bring to the church? What specific services might some undertake "for the sake of the reign of God"? What kinds of work, what sorts of actions for justice, might be particularly appropriate to, or flow from, the single Christian life? [3]

The community is incomplete without single people. This is true both because of the gifts and perspective singles bring, and also for their desire to be nurtured by the rest of the church. Yet, some singles really struggle with a sense of identity within the church. Who am I in the eyes of the community? And what is the role of an unmarried person in the context of a church? Clergy and community members sometimes look at singles and focus on what they do *not* have (for example, a spouse, children) as opposed to asking what singles *have* to offer and contribute to the life of the community.

There is a wonderful phrase that has been used to describe the challenge of working in multicultural congregations which says, "the house of God is holy not just because all are welcome there, but because all belong there."[4] I think the same can be said of single adults in parishes and communities where the majority of church membership is couples and families. The church is holy not because singles are welcome, but because they belong.

Belonging is more than membership in the way that someone belongs to the country club or a softball league. In the best sense of the word "belong," there is an innate sense that I really need to be here. It's a good fit. I deserve to be here, and my presence is missed when I'm absent. I *belong* here! Those who truly "belong" know that there is little distance between the newcomer and the longtime parishioner. Belonging is a way of saying to someone, "everything here is yours because you are one of us." It has nothing to do with membership or paying dues, but rather it is a shared sense of identity. When I experience a sense of belonging, I know that this is my spiritual home, my voice is heard, my needs are met, and my gifts are put to good use. The community understands my unique needs in terms of spirituality, formation, education, and prayer. Together there is a greater sense of responsibility to care for one another, and I can trust that my needs will be met in return. In the Christian community, we all belong, because we are one in Christ.

St. Paul writes an extended metaphor on the church as a body: "For just as the body is one and has many members, and all the members of the body, though many, are one body, so it is with Christ" (1 Corinthians 12:12). The church is *all* of us—infants, children, teens, young adults, singles, married couples, ordained priests, divorced individuals, widows, and widowers. Each brings their unique needs and contributions, but all make up one community, one body in Christ.

At times, we are so caught up in our individual needs and desires that we fail to recognize that we are also one contiguous body. Together we comprise the body of Christ; together we are formed with and shaped by one another. This unity in identity does not require uniformity in vocation or lifestyle choice. It does not mean we agree on everything or that we have the same interests. Surely we will not have the same background, and we each differ in our talents. Community is about being together, working together, and growing in faith together, often in spite of our differences.

In the context of community, both singles and couples need to recognize the many ways we depend upon one another. Couples and families provide single people with a model for fidelity, family, and love. They give singles an opportunity for ministry to and with children. Parents with young children model patience, compassion, forgiveness, and care. One's faith community can become a kind of extended "family" and provide a place to spend holidays if we cannot be with our own families.

Singles on the other hand offer a tremendous amount of time and dedication to the church. Many singles choose to share their talents through their volunteer commitments, fundraising efforts, maintenance of the building, and time for prayer. Single friends are a great source of fun, freedom, and carefree energy that is sometimes lost in the demands of family life. Single people also give witness to God's goodness in their lives through their openness, patience, and trust.

Community is essential to our Christian identity. As we embrace our separate roles within the community, we recognize God at work in our individual lives. We also discover God's presence as we depend on one another, pray with and for one another, support and challenge each other, minister to one another in times of need, and share in the sacraments together. At every stage of life, we have an opportunity to be the presence of Christ. Together, we *are* the body of Christ. As we grow as a community, it is a richer experience of Christ for all.

**Scripture to Remember**

Let the word of Christ dwell in you richly; teach and admonish one another in all wisdom; and with gratitude in your hearts sing psalms, hymns, and spiritual songs to God. And whatever you do, in word or deed, do everything in the name of the Lord Jesus, giving thanks to God the Father through him. (Colossians 3:16–17)

Now the whole group of those who believed were of one heart and soul, and no one claimed private ownership of any possessions, but everything they owned was held in common. With great power the apostles gave their testimony to the resurrection of the Lord Jesus, and great grace was upon them all. There was not a needy person among them, for as many as owned lands or houses sold them and brought the proceeds of what was sold. They laid it at the apostles' feet, and it was distributed to each as any had need. (Acts 4:32–35)

Now you are the body of Christ and individually members of it. And God has appointed in the church first apostles, second prophets, third teachers; then deeds of power, then gifts of healing, forms of assistance, forms of leadership, various kinds of tongues. Are all apostles? Are all prophets? Are all teachers? Do all work miracles? Do all possess gifts of healing? Do all speak in tongues? Do all interpret? But strive for the greater gifts. And I will show you a still more excellent way. (1 Corinthians 12:27–31)

**For Reflection**

1. What communities do I belong to? Who are the people that make up those communities with me? How do we care for, support, challenge, and affirm one another?
2. What has my experience been as an unmarried person in the context of a faith community? How have I been able to share my unique gifts and contribution with the church?
3. Do I sometimes fall into believing the myth that "if I *could* say yes, I *should* say yes" to everything? How do I decide when and where to share my time with the communities to which I belong?

**Try This ...**

- Set goals for finances, vacation, personal dreams, and review them regularly.
- Celebrate milestones and accomplishments that are important to you—birthdays, a promotion, an award, completing a marathon. Invite your friends and family to celebrate with you.
- The next time you are at a social function without a guest, make a point to introduce yourself to three new people. Find at least one thing you have in common with each of them.
- Make a list of your closest friends. What are the qualities you most appreciate in them? What keeps your friendship going? Is there anything missing or areas that could be improved? Write a letter to one person and tell them how much you appreciate their friendship.
- Write your own definition of success. Think beyond financial measurements. What are your personal benchmarks of progress? How will you know when you've made it? Consider how you spend you time, the people who surround you, and the ways you make a difference for others.
- Try this journal exercise. Make six columns with the following headings: Career, Family, Health/Exercise, Faith/Spirituality, Recreation/Fun, Volunteer Work. Under each column, write down how you spend time in each area. Are there any areas that seem out of balance? What do you need to give up in one area in order to gain more time in another area?
- Make a list of the various organizations and causes with whom you share your time, talent, treasure. Ask yourself: Is there a way that my giving could have a greater impact? Can I direct my talents in a more specific way? Can I afford to give more financially or donate money to a specific project? How does my dedication

of time make a difference—time spent building relationships, listening to other's concerns, praying for others?

- What do you need most from God in terms of being single? Make a list that begins "God, I really wish I had..." (more patience during the difficult moments, a greater appreciation for my friends, courage to take necessary risks, openness to finding a romantic partner, forgiveness for past mistakes, etc.) Each day, pick one item from your list and use it as a starting point for prayer.
- Practice Solitude. Spend ten or fifteen minutes a day sitting quietly in your favorite chair. Take a long walk through a nature preserve, along the beach, or in a local park. At first, it is likely that thoughts and distractions will pop into your mind. Try to let go of them without judgment. Be aware of your breathing, pay attention to your surroundings, and simply be still wherever you are.
- Spend some time getting to know the non-singles in your church community. Talk with newlyweds, parents, retired couples, widows, widowers. Ask them what is most exciting and most challenging about their current stage in life. Sometimes it's easier to feel a part of a community when we recognize that we share some of the same hopes, dreams, fears and struggles.
- Find a list of the ministries and volunteer opportunities at your local parish. Choose one thing that you care about, are good at doing, and that you enjoy. Then talk with someone about how you can get involved.

SECTION THREE

# Living Single With **Passion**

*Freedom*
*Love*
*Intimacy*
*Generativity*
*Hope*

CHAPTER TWELVE

# Living Single With **Freedom**

*Freedom consists not in doing what we like, but in having the right to do what we ought.*—Pope John Paul II[1]

## Combating Single Myth #12: **Singles Live a Carefree Life**

When asked what people enjoy most about being single, perhaps the most frequent response is the freedom that it brings. Freedom is one of the great joys of being single! While many singles look forward to the joys of marriage and the pride of parenthood, for this time in our lives (whether it is for now or forever), we relish in the vast sea of freedom that comes with having few obligations other than our own.

I am free to choose how I will spend my time, money, energy, and resources. I can make my own decisions about whether to stay in or go out. No one else can complain about how late I come home at night, if I decide to sleep in on weekends, or if I want to lounge in pajamas all day. There is a lot of satisfaction when making decisions regarding career changes, travel, and downtime that would be more complicated and difficult when in a relationship, especially one with children.

True freedom, however, does not equate to irresponsibility. Sure, I could stay up all night playing video games. I could eat cold pizza for breakfast. I could spend my weekends at the bar, the shopping mall, or the casino. Is that exercising my freedom? Yes. Is it responsible and good for my health? Not exactly.

Being single, especially choosing to be single, comes with a lot of risk and responsibility. If something in the condo needs repair or my car breaks down, it is my responsibility to fix it. If the stock market crashes and my 401(k) sinks, there isn't a second income to provide for me. If I get injured or laid off from work, my safety net is threaded together by my own choices about savings and insurance plans. I am responsible for everything, which can be liberating for some people and nerve-racking for others.

Regardless of our relationship status, life will never be completely free from worry or anxiety. True freedom compels us to make choices that reflect our fundamental values and outlook on life. We can choose to give back to our communities, be present for our families, pursue our careers with integrity, and devote time to our relationship with God. Freedom allows us to make choices consistent with God's call for our life, without the constant worry of making the wrong decision. Freedom allows us to move forward despite our fears.

Some of us are led to believe that single people have no worries at all or that our concerns are less important. Being single is fun and enjoyable, and we don't need to feel guilty about it! True freedom, however, calls us to exercise our responsibilities wisely, without being careless about how we go about it.

**Mind the Gap: Embracing the Pseudo-Single Life:::** *Christina Maria Paschyn*

For five years, since my junior year of college, I have been living in "pseudo-singlehood." I have been in a very long-distance relationship: My boyfriend lives in Scotland and I work in the United States.

In my international romance I struggle with the time difference, enormous flight costs, occasional pangs of loneliness and despair, as well as the overwhelming frustration I feel when I see other people enjoying face-to-face communication and intimacy.

Despite all my moaning, I enjoy being a pseudo-single woman. I have the best of both worlds: a boyfriend minus the annoyance of having to see him constantly and a single life sans the painfully awkward dates. But I assure you, my unorthodox relationship has been a blessing in disguise.

As my sorority sisters and college roommates struggled to balance their boyfriends' needs with their own interests and obligations, I faced no such challenge. I had the freedom to do what I wanted, when I wanted, without worrying about hurting the feelings of my man across the pond. While my girlfriends turned down social, travel, and job opportunities just to stay close to their flames, I followed my whims and dreams wherever they led me: from 1:00 AM house parties and auditions for traveling theater troupes to study programs and internships in Israel, Egypt, and beyond (with extended stops in Britain along the way!).

More significantly, unlike so many of my paired-off male and female friends, I learned to be at peace with myself. Single life allows for a gratifying amount of autonomy. Unfortunately, too many people fail to embrace this through no fault of their own. Our society bombards us with countless images of romantic love and sensationalist stories of "distraught" men and women who held off on marriage and children until it was "too late." Simply put, the pressure is constant.

This is where we pseudo-singles luck out: Stuck in a state of limbo between marriage and casual dating, we can approach the hysteria with a detached outsider's perspective. But don't believe the hype. Sure, wedding bells and baby carriages are wonderful stages in a person's life, but then again, so is singlehood. No other time allows a woman the opportunity to discover herself fully (emotionally, spiritually, and academically) or to figure out what she really wants in life.

I sometimes wonder how my life would have turned out if my boyfriend and I had lived in the same town during college. Would we have gotten married right after my graduation? And then, would I still have traveled around the world and experienced all the amazing things that I did? The point is I could not have asked for a better life journey. My adventures would not have been possible had I jumped into "wedded bliss" right away.

Yet our separate experiences and personal growth have only strengthened our resolve to be together. So now, as my boyfriend applies for his work visa to the United States, my pseudo-singlehood is destined to end. Perhaps marriage and children will be in our future. If it is, then I am confident we will succeed in it largely because we learned to be comfortable on our own first. Matrimony, we feel, should only enhance a couple's already strong bond and love for each other's unique and differing identities. Only then can two fully conscious and mature souls be united as one.

Single life has taught me that marriage is not an end in itself. A person can live an extremely fulfilling and meaningful existence without the added complexity brought on by a relationship. Indeed, while we are eager to start our lives together, there is a part of me that will miss that freedom when my love finally arrives here. But for those of you who hope to get hitched in the future, just remember to savor your single status now while you still can—otherwise, one day you may realize that you lived too little, too late.

**Spiritual Principle: Freedom**

Freedom is one of the greatest gifts of being single. But what does real freedom look like in the single life? How do we know that we are acting in a way that is truly free?

Some people consider freedom as permission to do or say whatever they want without any regard for how their actions or decisions will impact others. Sure, we have endless choices about how to spend our lives, barring any financial constraints, personal obligations, and consequences of previous choices. But freedom is more than carefree living, creative self-expression, and uninhibited risk-taking. When we are truly free, we are compelled to act in accordance with our deepest values and inner truth. True freedom allows us to be the person God intends us to be.

Freedom begins with authentic discernment and results in taking a risk. Discernment is a process of prayerful decision making, knowing that God cares about our decisions, asking God to show us all the possible alternatives, and believing that God will guide us to make the best choice. This includes gathering information, weighing our options, paying attention to the interior movements of our hearts, talking to people who know us well, accepting the things we cannot change about our situation, and finally moving forward with a decision. These steps take time, and we don't do them all at once. Ideally, discernment is done in the context of prayer and with the support of friends, family, and one's faith community.

The opposite of freedom is to be dependent on or attached to someone or something in an unhealthy manner. When we are not free, we are usually focused too much on ourselves or trying to live up to other people's expectations. Instead of allowing our decisions to flow from a place of authentic discernment, those who are not free tend to make decisions by obligation or default. Those who make decisions out of an unhealthy sense of obligation do so from a place of guilt, remorse, or feeling like "I owe something" to another person. Those who make decisions by default often settle for less than the best that life has to offer because they think there is nothing better or cannot imagine their circumstances in any other way. Neither way is fulfilling and can lead to resentment, anger, or a loss of one's sense of self.

Freedom is also impeded by fear. Our freedom of speech is hindered when there is fear of rejection or criticism. Our longing to follow our wildest dreams can be halted by a fear of failure or pressure to meet someone else's expectations. However, freedom also comes with a certain amount of necessary fear. A healthy sense of fear protects us from getting hurt, physically or emotionally, and it reminds us to take necessary precautions. When our risks are preceded by an appropriate amount of discernment, we generally find ourselves more willing to respond to God's call, even if that means stepping outside our comfort zone. Those who are truly free can act in accordance with God's call, even in the face of fear.

Finally, true freedom requires that we be willing to take risks. I'm not talking about the kind of risk-taking that is reckless or irresponsible, rather, to risk is to live boldly. Risks stretch us to become more of who God intends us to be. This might include going back to school, making a career change or geographical move, or entering into a serious relationship with another. We find ourselves saying, "I'm not exactly sure how this is going to turn out, but I'm willing to trust God has good things in store for me."

Risks require a tremendous amount of faith and trust. Those who take pleasure being single know that the single life comes with a tremendous amount of freedom. In order to truly enjoy that freedom, we have to be prepared for the risks and responsibilities that accompany it. Discernment assures that our freedom is used in a responsible manner, it puts our fears into perspective, and releases us from pressures placed upon us by family, friends, and society at large. Ultimately, freedom gives us the courage to live as God intends.

**Scripture to Remember**

Therefore I tell you, do not worry about your life, what you will eat or what you will drink, or about your body, what you will wear. Is not life more than food, and the body more than clothing? (Matthew 6:25)

For you were called to freedom, brothers and sisters; only do not use your freedom as an opportunity for self-indulgence, but through love become slaves to one another. (Galatians 5:13)

**For Reflection**

1. How do I exercise freedom in my single life? With whom do I share my freedom? What are the commitments I have made out of a sense of freedom?
2. Under what situations or circumstances do I find myself less free? Where do I wish to be more free in my life?
3. Are there areas of my life in which my freedom is impeded by fear? What am I afraid of and where am I being challenged to take more risks?

CHAPTER THIRTEEN

# Living Single With **Love**

*I think one of the most commonly held misperceptions is that an active dating life is essential to preparing one's self for marriage, as though love and marriage require their own skill set acquired only through their own pursuit. Rather, I've come to believe that relationships require us to call upon all that we know, and my season as a single person has helped me to build up and integrate all that I am.* –Lisa, 29

## Combating Single Myth #13: **The More Singles Date, the More They Increase Their Chances**

Consciously or not, many singles find themselves on a continual quest to find that special someone. Ask any unmarried person "What are you looking for?" and I suspect they will respond with a well thought-out list of qualities that they seek or avoid in a romantic relationship. How many of us have such a list in our minds, if not on paper? I once created an inventory that included physical attributes, interpersonal traits, extracurricular activities, family commitments, and spiritual values. When it comes to searching for a mate, we presume to know what is best. Yet, one of the best pieces of dating advice I received from my sister-in-law was this, "Do not eliminate someone simply because he does not meet all the criteria on your list. Ultimately, God gives us what we *need* in a relationship, which is not always the same as what we think we *want*."

The power of the Internet has taken dating to a whole new level. Once considered taboo, I know more and more people who have met their perfect match online. But online dating comes with its advantages and challenges. Potential partners have an opportunity to get to know one another before ever meeting face to face. For better or worse, much of the "small talk" that happens early in a relationship may already be included in their profile. Perhaps we rule out some people too quickly because they don't meet all of our criteria. And while we hope that people will be sincere in describing themselves, there are some who knowingly stretch the truth. Singles are mystified when the person we "meet" online does not fit the description of the one who walks through the door on the first date.

Online dating has truly run amok in situations where finding the "perfect" match becomes an obsession. If we're not careful, romance can be reduced to the same level as a retail shopping spree. Meeting the man or woman with whom you'd like to spend the rest of your life is not the same as buying a new car or trying on a cocktail dress.

Yet there is a subtle temptation to make superficial judgments about a person or market ourselves to stand out above the rest. When we are focused solely on who makes the cut and who does not, we fail to see people for who they truly are–made in the image and likeness of God, with gifts and limitations, like each one of us. Furthermore, singles can spend hours sifting through profiles (sometimes with great frustration and little luck) when they could be engaging with real people or doing things they enjoy. If we are simply "shopping" for the ideal partner, it is easy to forget that relationships are messy and people aren't perfect. Each one of us comes with a story, personality, family, feelings, and so much more that you can't see through a computer screen.

Singles are often told, "the more you date the more you increase the chances of meeting the one with whom you will spend the rest of your life." Is this a myth or a sound approach to finding your soul mate? Those in favor of an active dating life contend that dating is a great way to get to know a wide variety of people, to understand ourselves in relationship to others, and to more readily recognize "the one" when he or she appears. On the other hand, is it enough to be single and not actively pursuing a partner? What are you *really* looking for?

**Stirred to Love:::** *Allison Leigh*

I loathe the idea of marriage as a goal. I watch the character Charlotte on the television show *Sex and the City* when she proclaims she is going to be married that year, and I cringe. She does indeed get married, and it doesn't work out. Long before her example, this idea of being married by a certain age or time bothered me. It gives me the same reaction as nails on a chalkboard; I close my eyes and turn away.

I am a goal-oriented person. I love timelines, plans, schedules, and checklists. I use them every day at work; I use races and training plans as motivation for exercise; I make grocery lists. So why is the idea of marriage as a goal repulsive to me?

St. Teresa of Avila said, "[T]he important thing is not to think much but to love much; and so to do that which best stirs you to love. Perhaps we don't know what love is. I wouldn't be very much surprised, because it doesn't consist in great delight but in desiring with strong determination to please God in everything...".[1] Do that which best stirs you to love. Isn't marriage supposed to be all about love? Since when does love follow a timeline?

A friend of mine recently tried to convince me to try online dating. Any unmarried person in their thirties has probably heard the spiel about online dating from well-intentioned friends. I try to avoid it. I avoid it by doing what brings me joy: my work, running a marathon, spending time with my friends, helping other people whenever I can. I also never utter complaints about being single or wish out loud to be in a relationship. It just isn't something I'm sure I want.

This conversation about dating was unsettling to me for a couple of reasons. First, it was clear that this "friend" of mine really didn't know me well. She assumed and even suggested that I have a goal of being a wife and mother. And she implied that my life is incomplete since I am not married. Yet another cause for concern is that online dating, to me, feels like treating marriage (or at least a romantic relationship) as a goal. No relationship in my life, be it great friends or boyfriends, has ever come to me in a way that I planned or contrived. Those great relationships have happened because I am open to love wherever and however it finds me. Those great experiences of love have not matched a checklist or profile I might have had.

Some tell me I will never be married if I don't "get out there." What does that even mean? My first response is, "Would that be so bad?" I am blessed beyond measure in my life. I feel the love of God all around me and have freedom to pursue the things that bring me joy.

My second response is if "out there" means things like singles bars and online dating, then those things just don't stir me to love. It isn't that I don't wish to be in a romantic relationship sometimes. (In the same way, I am guessing, some married people long for their single days again.) I do want to be the most important person in someone's life and have that same person be the most important person in mine, but I don't want marriage to be about a plan. I want to be so swept up in a love I can't explain that marriage is the only choice. I want to be in a relationship because it stirs me to love.

I don't have a goal of getting married, I desire love: to love much and to be loved. Aiming for marriage feels like bypassing the love that leads to it. God's love is a powerful and mysterious thing that I have come to trust in. My prayer is that God will help me do that which leads me to love. Maybe one day that will lead me to get married. Maybe it won't. But if there is a goal I want to pursue, it's bigger even than marriage. It's finding and living in love.

**Spiritual Principle: Love**

At a certain point, most singles move beyond the desire for a fairy-tale romance. We know that even the ideal relationship is not picture perfect. Love is more than adolescent infatuation, physical attraction, and egocentric desire. The best of couples will tell you that life is full of surprises and nothing ever goes exactly as planned. Happily ever after is sure to include dishes, diapers, financial difficulties, and the occasional disagreement. Love means that we do not have to be perfect all of the time.

Yet many of us live with the notion that our desire for love can only be filled by a soul mate, a true companion, a best friend. We long to know another and to be known by someone. We desire to find that one person with whom we can share intimate details, who will be excited to hear about our day, with whom we can be our true selves, someone to have fun with and share common interests. We desire to be known inside and out, to be supported through tragedy and celebration, through illness and unto death.

What we long for is love. At times we try to fill that emptiness with many other things. Love fails when it turns inward toward ourselves, when we attempt to fill the need for love with endless amounts of food, drink, exercise, Internet, pornography, excessive religiosity, gambling, or thrill-seeking. Selfish loves fail to satisfy. When our impetus for love is to garner attention, to only feel good about ourselves, or to get noticed by others we are left unsatisfied.

The Scriptures tell us that God is love (1 John 4:8). As human creatures, made in God's image, God's love is etched on our hearts. We were created in love, for love, by a God who is love. Love has left its fingerprints on us, and love alone is what satisfies the emptiness in our hearts. All love comes from God and is directed toward God. The desire to give and receive love is one of the most authentic and natural desires; for where there is true love, there is God.

So often we have been taught that the ideal place (or only place) to experience God's love is through the sacred bond of marriage. Indeed, married love is a reflection of God's love, and God's love is vividly experienced in healthy and holy marriages. As a sacrament, marriage makes visible the invisible grace of God, and God's love becomes present by the love shared between a husband and a wife. But, is marriage the only place where God's love is experienced in its fullness? Of course not! God is not selfish. God does not reserve love only to those who are married. God does not withhold love from single people. It is possible to know God's deep and abiding love in other ways.

As single people, we long for the radical commitment that draws us into intimate relationship with another, but there is a significant difference in the way those relationships are lived out. What does a single person's love look like?

Love is experienced in the closeness of friendship. Love is shown in the sacrifices we make for our families. Love is poured out in the generosity of service and stewardship. Our lives become a witness to God's love through prayer and interaction with our faith communities. Any healthy and committed relationship requires a considerable amount of honesty, trust, acceptance, forgiveness, and sacrifice. Furthermore, there is more love when you give it away. We experience and receive more love when it is *given* than when it is kept to oneself.

Jesus says, "This is my commandment, that you love one another as I have loved you. No one has greater love than this, to lay down one's life for one's friends" (John 15:12–13). This is our fundamental call as Christians—to love one another. How can we take Jesus' command and apply it to our singleness? What does it mean to experience love by laying down our lives?

Love that lays down its life for another is experienced in service to the poor, in commitment to our families, and through the joy of friendship. When we willingly lay down our lives for others, love makes demands on us. Love makes us forget about ourselves and think more about the people we serve and care about. Laying down one's life may include setting aside expectations, making sacrifices of time or money, accepting another person's faults, or going out of one's way to help another. Laying down one's life means learning how to express our fears and expectations, communicating our concerns, and setting healthy boundaries. Laying down one's life means fighting fair and learning to forgive. In this way, love extends beyond infatuation and is much bigger than any romantic relationship.

It is possible to be in love without being in a romantic relationship. Consider the people, causes, and situations in which you are willing to sacrifice your time, money, and resources. Where do you allow yourself to be inconvenienced without complaint to ensure the safety, success, or well being of another? We sacrifice ourselves for our family, friends, and faith community. We give ourselves over in prayer, in volunteer service, in civic engagement, and in support of those who are most in need. This kind of radical commitment can come as a threat to our independent single lives, but the places where we are most fully committed are likely the places we are most fully in love. When we engage in relationships that are built on committed sacrificial love, it is there that we meet God. And God alone fills the emptiness and longing of our hearts.

**Scripture to Remember**

One of the scribes came near and heard them disputing with one another, and seeing that he answered them well, he asked him, "Which commandment is the first of all?" Jesus answered, "The first is, 'Hear, O Israel: the Lord our God, the Lord is one; you shall love the Lord your God with all your heart, and with all your soul, and with all your mind, and with all your strength.' The second is this, 'You shall love your neighbor as yourself.' There is no other commandment greater than these." (Mark 12:28–31)

Love is patient; love is kind; love is not envious or boastful or arrogant or rude. It does not insist on its own way; it is not irritable or resentful; it does not rejoice in wrongdoing, but rejoices in the truth. It bears all things, believes all things, hopes all things, endures all things. (1 Corinthians 13:4–7)

As God's chosen ones, holy and beloved, clothe yourselves with compassion, kindness, humility, meekness, and patience. Bear with one another and, if anyone has a complaint against another, forgive each other; just as the Lord has forgiven you, so you also must forgive. Above all, clothe yourselves with love, which binds everything together in perfect harmony. (Colossians 3:12–14)

**For Reflection**

1. What do I seek most in my relationships with others? How will I know when I've found it?
2. Where is God's love most present and visible in my life? How does God's love influence my relationships with others?
3. To whom or to what am I most fully committed? Where do I make sacrifices for the sake of others? How do I share my love and in what ways is love returned to me?

## CHAPTER FOURTEEN

# Living Single With **Intimacy**

*To lose oneself in another person's arms, or in another person's company, or in compassionate solidarity with all who suffer, is to find one's truest identity as a human person. In the end, these are not as much different kinds of loving as they are diverse expressions of the same sacred energy.* —Fran Ferder and John Heagle[1]

## Combating Single Myth #14: **Sex–Everyone is Doing It**

She leaned over the table and discreetly whispered, "Are you a virgin?" I felt the twinge of adolescent awkwardness, even though I was conversing with one of my best girlfriends. We'd been friends for several years, and I'd been single the entire time, so it was a subject that had never come up until now. As best friends do from time to time, we were recounting secret crushes, lost loves, second chances, and mistakes we'd both made. The pang in my chest reminded me that being content with singlehood did not happen overnight. Even more, our conversation reminded me once again that sexuality is a sensitive subject, even when it's discussed between good friends.

When it comes to stereotypes and assumptions about single people, questions about sex and sexuality top the list! We live in a "hookup" culture where sex has become more recreational than it is relational. In many instances, sex is a stepping stone into a relationship instead of a response to an established loving commitment made in marriage. There is a stereotype that being single equals sleeping around, and if you're not willing to sleep with someone, then you must be coldhearted or asexual. Attached to this myth is the perception that everyone has sex on the third date (not true), and that having sex is the only way to satisfy your need for intimacy (also not true).

The social acceptance of sex outside of marriage is a huge obstacle for many singles. Do I give in to the pressure? Will I be judged if I tell someone I'm a virgin or not a virgin? Where do I draw the line in physical intimacy, and will I risk rejection? How do I communicate my desire to be with someone in an intimate way and still maintain healthy boundaries? Furthermore, how do I respond to genuine arousal in a normal and healthy way, whether I'm in a relationship or not?

Similarly, questions or presumptions about sexual orientation can be a complicated and sensitive subject. In regards to being single, my sister once asked me, "Are you sure you're not a lesbian?" Followed by, "I'd still love you if you are." I'm not gay, but I think my sister held onto an uncanny hope that I would come out of the closet or at least confide in her more often during this extended dating dry spell. Had she forgotten about all the guys I dated in high school and college? What bothered me more than anything else was that I needed some valid excuse for why I wasn't dating anyone. It seemed like an affirmative response to the question, "Are you gay?" would have been more acceptable than "all the good ones are taken." Even my sarcastic standby, "But Jesus was single..." didn't quite fly with her.

I shared this story with a number of friends, who assured me that I am not the only unmarried person who has been the focal point of such a conversation. Most of us look back on those moments and laugh. But there are many individuals for whom sexual identity is a profound and legitimate struggle. Such questions or accusations from family or friends may result in additional embarrassment, shame, or continued denial of one's sexual identity.

Understanding ourselves as sexual beings is a real mark of maturity, especially in a culture where sex is often reduced to physical pleasure. Our sexuality is a natural and healthy part of how God made us. Sex is a gift! It is a gift God gives to us as part of ourselves, and it is a precious gift that we give to one another meant to express love and bring life into the world. The more we see ourselves as sexual beings made for intimacy with one another, the better we are able to integrate a healthy sexuality into our single lives.

**A Touching Story:::** *Lisa Furney*

There is certainly a perception in our culture that everyone is having sex, especially "those single folks" who must be having rampant casual sex and enjoying every minute of it! Although it is hard to maintain a certain lifestyle, remaining a virgin until marriage is still a worthwhile endeavor! This may seem like a strange undertaking for some, who see the choice to remain abstinent as absurd or old-fashioned. Yet, even singles that are committed to this countercultural way of life long for a connection and crave physical contact with other people.

I once explained to a married friend that singles tend to go through times of being touch-deprived, especially for those of us who are touchy-feely people. This is not necessarily sex-related. I just mean touch in general. People in families have the gift of touch bestowed upon them in many forms, such as: playing with little children, holding hands while crossing the street, picking up a crying baby, being grabbed around the legs by a child, cuddling on the couch while watching a movie, and kissing your kids or spouse goodnight.

In whatever form it may take (and whether it is wanted or not), the married person has ample instances of "touch." A single person could go for days or weeks without a simple pat on the back, touch on the arm, or a hug. These are very meaningful ways of expressing ourselves, and it can be detrimental for a single person to be deprived of that over long periods of time. One of the gifts of friendship comes in being able to satisfy the need for touch by hugging our friends.

Sexual intercourse is not the only way to fulfill that desire for closeness and physical affection. Yet singles who wait to have sex are sometimes viewed as having something wrong with them. One person tried to sway me by saying, "God created pleasure too, you know!" Yes, He did but it was meant for the right context, within a committed marriage relationship, not just as a "get it while you can" phenomenon. In another instance, an ex-boyfriend said that he had a hard time seeing me as a "sexual being" simply because I hadn't experienced sex yet. When we wait to have sex and with that one special person, it can be a beautiful gift from God.

Close friendships also satisfy our need for intimacy, not in terms of sexual needs obviously, but in terms of reaching out and truly connecting with another person, sharing our heart and soul with one another, being open and honest with our thoughts and feelings, being loved for who we are as God's children. I have been blessed by many such friendships. They have helped me through tough times and celebrated with me in joyous times too. They bestow on me the gift of touch and fill a need for healthy intimacy in my life.

## Spiritual Principle: Intimacy

One key to an abundant and fulfilling single life is understanding ourselves as sexual beings. This includes our needs for physical affection and emotional intimacy. I grew up with a "just say no" approach to sex, a helpful guideline to me as an adolescent learning to set healthy boundaries at a time of physical change and emotional uncertainty. But those lessons became less effective as a mature adult hoping to integrate sexuality and intimacy into day-to-day relationships.

For the unmarried person, it is essential that we understand our need for intimacy and establish a means of channeling that intimacy in positive ways. Intimacy, the experience of being up close and personal with another, takes on many different forms in both romantic and non-romantic settings. Sexual intimacy, engaging in genital sex, or sharing in physical pleasure, is only one type of intimacy. Consider the closeness we feel with someone when we share in the world of ideas (intellectual intimacy), the relationships that form when we share experiences of fun and play (recreational intimacy), and the unity that results from shared religious expression or time spent together in prayer (spiritual intimacy).

Furthermore, many people crave emotional intimacy, whether from a lover, a sister, or a best friend who knows us at the core of who we are. We want someone with whom we can share our secrets, vent our frustrations, and confess our joy. Often we confuse this need for emotional intimacy with a desire for physical affection. We think we want sex when what we really long for is a deep and lasting emotional connection.

When it comes to achieving that sense of closeness with another, we all have different needs and degrees of satisfaction. For singles, especially those not engaged in a romantic relationship, we should consider how our intimacy needs can be met in other ways.

Some people feel most fulfilled by giving and receiving physical affection, and it's good for us to seek an appropriate outlet for this.

My friend Angela, from a big Italian family, is naturally affectionate and generously shares hugs and kisses on the cheek. She is someone I can always turn to when I am in need of a warm embrace.

In similar ways, it is important to find people and places where we are fulfilled in our need for intellectual stimulation, rewarding work, spiritual connection, and experiences of fun and recreation.

Another big question for single adults revolves around physical desire, healthy sexual attraction, and response to genuine arousal, whether that is in the context of a romantic relationship or not. For those of us who grew up thinking that sexual feelings are bad, we sometimes approach these situations with the mindset that we need to stop, avoid, or somehow shut off those feelings.

There are certain situations to avoid, like engaging in the hookup culture for the sole purpose of selfish pleasure, viewing pornography (in print, film, or on the Internet), or frequenting strip clubs. To a certain extent, we might also monitor the books and magazines we read and the movies we view. When we intentionally engage our sexual imagination, we often fuel selfish desires, and we may be tempted to resolve that sexual tension in unhealthy or immoral ways.

On the other hand, there are a number of situations where attraction and arousal is a normal response. Perhaps I meet someone for the first time and find myself physically or emotionally attracted to this person. Moments of intense intimacy, even those of a non-physical nature, may prompt a rise in body temperature, our heartbeat quickens, and we recognize our body's natural response. We can't always predict when this will happen, and there is no need to suppress these authentic reactions.

How do we integrate a healthy sense of sexuality into our lives? Begin by acknowledging that this is a normal part of who God made you to be. Admit your feelings and decide an appropriate way to express them. Ask yourself, "Are my signs of physical affection consistent with the level of commitment in the relationship?" Ideally, sexual intercourse is reserved for marriage because it is an expression of total, complete surrender and commitment to another. As a single person, are there other ways you can communicate your care, desire, and commitment?

Finally, allow yourself to bring this part of your life into prayer. Often sexuality is something we reserve to sharing in secret with our best friend, and many people cannot imagine talking with God about it. Tell God what it feels like to be you. Share with God what you enjoy about your relationships and what seems to be missing from them. Ask yourself if there are types of intimacy (physical, emotional, recreational, or spiritual) that are not being satisfied, then ask God to show you where those needs can be fulfilled.

Especially for those who are committed to living single, chaste, or celibate lives, we need to integrate sexuality and intimacy into our lives in healthy and holy ways. This doesn't happen by suppressing, ignoring, or pretending that sexual feelings don't exist. Healthy sexual integration is a lot of work. It takes a concerted amount of self-reflection, honest communication, and prayer, and we will likely make some mistakes along the way. But for the single individual, it is ultimately the path to sharing our love.

**Scripture to Remember**

Let all that you do be done in love. (1 Corinthians 16:14)

By contrast, the fruit of the Spirit is love, joy, peace, patience, kindness, generosity, faithfulness, gentleness, and self-control. There is no law against such things. And those who belong to Christ Jesus have crucified the flesh with its passions and desires. If we live by the Spirit, let us also be guided by the Spirit. (Galatians 5:22–25)

Finally, beloved, whatever is true, whatever is honorable, whatever is just, whatever is pure, whatever is pleasing, whatever is commendable, if there is any excellence and if there is anything worthy of praise, think about these things. Keep on doing the things that you have learned and received and heard and seen in me, and the God of peace will be with you. (Philippians 4:8–9)

**For Reflection**

1. We all have a need for attention and affection, both physical and emotional. What does a healthy sense of intimacy look like in my life?
2. How are my needs for physical, emotional, recreational, and spiritual intimacy being fulfilled? What types of intimacy are missing from my life?
3. Who are the people that I call upon for emotional intimacy, intellectual intimacy, and spiritual intimacy? How would I describe the "closeness" that I feel with them?

CHAPTER FIFTEEN

# Living Single and **Generativity**

*I don't want to be a spinster living alone with a rocking chair and eighteen cats.*—Alison, 33

## Combating Single Myth #15: **If I Don't Get Married Soon, I Will Never Have Children**

My friend Michelle is a doctor who has worked for many years in a family practice clinic. She is well informed about the importance of prenatal care for expectant mothers at any age, but as a general rule of thumb, any pregnant woman over age thirty-five is considered a high-risk patient. While women continue to have healthy pregnancies into their forties, I know a number of women who have panicked at the prospect of turning thirty knowing that they have five "good years" left on the clock. Michelle herself once told me, "By the time I nearly hit thirty-five, I knew that marriage and children were not in my immediate future. I spent the days leading up to my birthday in a deep, dark funk. Great, I'm thirty-five and single, now what?"

There is something instinctive about the desire to have children. I know men who look forward to fatherhood and raising a family, and women who crave the feeling of holding a baby in their arms. Perhaps women are more attuned to the signs that their bodies are changing and more aware that Mother Nature has a time limit on our ability to bear biological children. For many of us, men and women, there is something mesmerizing about a baby that makes us want to stop and stare.

For the single person, especially when marriage and children are not on the immediate horizon, it is not uncommon to wonder how God is using our lives to create new life for the future. What if I never have biological children? Can my life be complete without a traditional family? Frightening as it may seem, these are important questions, especially for people who feel called to be intentionally single, for individuals beyond their child bearing years, and for singles for whom marriage and family appear to be a long way off.

There are many ways to parent and nurture the next generation. Life-giving relationships happen through mentoring, coaching, teaching, friendship, helping professions, and spending time with our nieces and nephews. There are some individuals who find themselves as single parents or choose to pursue childbirth or adoption on their own. But for the vast majority of singles, bringing new life into the world requires that we be creative and generative in bold and imaginative ways! Sometimes what we need is a shift in perspective, especially when the biological clock starts ticking.

**A Runner's Love:::** *Joanne Singleton*

When I was little, I watched television, read magazines, and sang popular songs that reassured me one day I would meet a man, fall in love, and live happily ever after. I assumed that I would only know and experience love once marriage was on the horizon. Today I am thirty-eight, single, very happy, and am discovering I can be "in love" without being in a romantic relationship. I am also learning that being in love with God is the priority of my life.

However, some days I struggle to trust God and I question if I really am content with my single life. This generally happens when someone asks, "Are you married?" The truth is as a single person I feel fulfilled and am not living a lonely, boring life. I have many friends, married and single, who enrich my life and challenge me to discover how I can use my gifts and talents for the greater glory of God. Love, I have discovered, does not just exist in the marriages of films and pop records of my youth.

I have experienced love when I run, when I challenge myself and others to go to the very limits of our physical selves. The gift of running has changed my life and the lives of people around me, in ways that I could never have imagined.

Brianna is my niece, well, actually the niece of my best friend, who is like a sister to me. Several years ago, on the day before a visit, I got a phone call from Brianna's mom who told me that Brianna's best friend had died unexpectedly. She said it was all right if I postponed the trip. Of course, I went and even extended my stay to be present through the services.

When I arrived, Brianna seemed distant, understandably heartbroken by her loss. Her parents worried and struggled to help. Professionally I am a social worker, but this was personal, and I wanted to offer perfect answers for painful questions, to provide some comfort in the midst of such sorrow.

Thankfully, I was in the middle of training for my first Boston marathon. My long run that weekend entailed seventeen miles, perfect for a long conversation with God. The wind was strong, the air chilly, and the gravel road seemed to go on forever. I spent much of the run thinking how unfair life is, struggling to pray. But the longer I ran and the more exhausted I became, the easier it seemed to let go of my own thoughts and allow God into that space. And as God's presence grew, so did my understanding of how training and running a marathon are like the journey of life. Through prayer, I found insight into how my running could help Brianna: She deserved a medal for what she was enduring, so why not give her my Boston marathon medal?

When I returned home, I continued my training, and when race day came, I ran, finding strength when the hills got hard, knowing how much I wanted Brianna to know that I loved and cared for her. I ran knowing my pain was short-lived, hoping the medal I would earn would help in some small way to ease Brianna's pain. When I finished, I was given a lovely blue and yellow medal. One month later, I gave Brianna her medal.

God has gifted me with many things: loving family and friends, the ability to run, a job that I love. I truly believe that being single is also a gift. Through this gift I have learned who I am and how I can be part of other's lives in a meaningful way. I have been given amazing opportunities to build relationships that may not have flourished had I been married with children. God has presented a way for me to live my life and love others that may seem less than orthodox. Yet as long as I know I am fulfilling God's purpose for my life, I shall continue to enjoy God's call to be single.

### Spiritual Principle: Generativity

Several years ago, I stopped into a pottery studio and a striking red vase caught my eye. The artist noticed my gaze and gently pulled the vase off the top shelf for me. He explained that the deep red color was one-of-a-kind, the natural clay in the area taking on a beautiful brown and occasionally a bright blue when fired. The red is very rare, he explained. It takes the right combination of oxygen, air pockets, fire temperature, and distribution of heat in the oven. I could not recreate this vase, even if I tried, he said.

I often imagine that God looks upon humankind much like the artist who fashioned that vase from the clay of the earth. Ever so gently God holds creation and says, "You are a rare beauty, one of a kind. I could not recreate you, even if I tried." There are many images in Scripture that portray God as creator, potter, and artist. The psalmist pays tribute to God who formed our inmost being and shaped our days before a single one came to be (Psalm 139:13–16). The wisdom of Sirach reminds us, "He molds the clay with his arm / and makes it pliable with his feet; / he sets his heart on finishing the glazing, and he takes care in firing the kiln" (38:30). Our lives are like clay, pliable and soft in the hands of God, molded for God's purpose, and etched by the Master's design. The prophet Isaiah extols, "Yet, O LORD, you are our Father; / we are the clay, and you are our potter; / we are all the work of your hand." (64:8).

God, who first breathed life into us at the beginning of time, is the ultimate Artist. The Creator loves creating. It is in God's very nature to be generative. As children of the Artist, we all have inherent creative instincts. For some, these gifts are manifested in the traditional arts like music, sculpture, creative writing, painting, and dance. Others find themselves engaged in work that directly touches the lives of others through teaching, counseling, health care, or ministry. There is also a certain artistry to the scientific study of chemistry, biology, mathematics, and engineering, especially when those skills lead to new discoveries that benefit all of society.

Our creative energies send new life flowing forth from our bodies, our lives, our work, our relationships, and other innovative enterprises. Being single does not negate this very natural part of our humanity. As single people, it is important that we find an outlet for being generative in order to fulfill that hope and desire that our activities and relationships become life-giving for others. Singles need to be encouraged to embrace the creative part of themselves and act upon those longings. Who or what are you breathing life into? Where is God inviting you to use your creative powers to their fullest potential?

Another way to ask this question is to consider, "How is my outreach to others 'giving birth' to something new in the world?" New life expresses itself by welcoming guests into your home, creating works of art, visiting a sick friend in the hospital, bringing joy to people through the gift of music, or spending time in prayer. We bring forth new life into the world when we mentor new employees, care for the ill or the elderly, teach young children, and provide financial support to worthwhile causes. New life comes through prayer, through volunteer service, and through relationships with the poor. It happens in chapels and soup kitchens and hospital rooms.

For many singles, the realization that having biological children is not probable (or even impossible) can be quite disheartening and leave us wondering where there is meaning and fulfillment in life. In these times, it is even more important that we name and celebrate the experiences in which we are nurturing, caring, protecting, and providing for the next generation. This is important both for those who will never marry and those who may marry after they are beyond their child bearing years. What do community and family look like for me as a single person? Who are my children? Who makes up my family in addition to my biological relatives? God does not place in us that call to nurture and care for others and then leave it an empty void.

One key to a fulfilling single life is to take time to identify and celebrate the many ways, with or without children, that we create new life and leave a legacy for those who follow us. The spiritual challenge is to see the hand of God at work and to appreciate the new life that God is creating through our presence. Where is new life coming forth from your work and your place in the world?

**Scripture to Remember**

[G]ive, and it will be given to you. A good measure, pressed down, shaken together, running over, will be put into your lap; for the measure you give will be the measure you get back. (Luke 6:38)

Abide in me as I abide in you. Just as the branch cannot bear fruit by itself unless it abides in the vine, neither can you unless you abide in me. I am the vine, you are the branches. Those who abide in me and I in them bear much fruit, because apart from me you can do nothing. (John 15:4–5)

Rejoice in hope, be patient in suffering, persevere in prayer. Contribute to the needs of the saints; extend hospitality to strangers. Bless those who persecute you; bless and do not curse them. Rejoice with those who rejoice, weep with those who weep. Live in harmony with one another; do not be haughty, but associate with the lowly; do not claim to be wiser than you are. (Romans 12:12–16)

**For Reflection**

1. Can I entertain the idea that I might have a full and complete life without dating, marriage, or biological children? If so, what would that look like?
2. What is the legacy I wish to leave behind? Who will be the recipient of this? How will I be remembered and known by the next generation?

3. How do my gifts, skills, hobbies, and interests bring a sense of joy and fulfillment to others? How am I creating new life in bold and faithful ways?

CHAPTER SIXTEEN

# Living Single With **Hope**

*It is much better to be single and searching than married and hurting.*—Brad, 29

## Combating Single Myth #16: **If We Break Up, There Will Never Be Another**

A wise priest once told me that it is good to get angry with God every once in a while. "Really?" I replied, "It's *good* to get angry with God?"

Anger brings clarity to the things we most value. We get angry when the things we truly care about are threatened, whether that means losing a heated argument or the fear of losing a close friend. We get angry in our attempts to save our pride, when we stand up for what we believe, or in the face of injustice. Anger exposes our passion for another person or for a particular cause. When we allow ourselves to be angry at God, we reveal those places that are most raw and vulnerable, and allow ourselves to be fully known. Some of the most compelling prayers are those in which we hurl our hurts back at God with gut-wrenching honesty. God can handle it because God alone knows the source of our anger, and God will continue to love us in a way that only God knows how.

I remembered this bit of advice one Saturday night after a day of celebrating the wedding of a good friend. I cannot imagine two people more perfect for one another. It was a beautiful ceremony and delicious meal, followed by live music and dancing into the wee hours of the night. Every last detail was accounted for. The calligraphy on the invitations matched the place cards at our seats, there were flower petals scattered on every table, and party favors with a personalized message from the bride and groom. This wedding included everything I had always imagined for myself, but there was only one problem: It wasn't mine.

It seemed as if God was withholding all these things from me, and I was no longer willing to hold back. Once at home I threw my purse on the floor, flung my heels off and sent them flying across the room. I flopped myself down on the bed and shouted at the ceiling, "I hate you! How could you let this happen? Why does everyone else get to be happy?"

Granted, my last serious relationship had ended nearly a year before. And although I was truly happy for my friends, their day of nuptial bliss had triggered a deep well of sadness, anger, and jealousy. I felt hopeless and certain that I would never find love again.

You cannot force a happily-ever-after ending on a relationship that wasn't meant to be. Every relationship has its ups and downs, but when things get tough, we invariably ask, "Is this an invitation to greater self-awareness, an opportunity for us to improve our skills as a couple, or is this the final warning sign that I should leave?"

We probably all know couples who tough it out too long, and others who throw in the towel much too soon. Maybe you called it quits after a few months, or find yourself waning after several years in a serious relationship. As our dreams of a possible match made in heaven die, one lingering question remains, "If we break up, will there ever be another?"

**Fasting Forward:::** *Megan Sweas*

I stared at the e-mail to my ex, wondering whether to push "send." "How are you?" he had asked. "I'm fine. Quite a snowstorm you guys got out east," I responded, as if all my dreams for the future—jobs in the same city, then marriage, eventually a family—hadn't crashed two weeks before, the last time we talked. Three years of a long-distance relationship was over, leaving me scared and lonely, wondering "Now what?"

"Do I keep talking with him?" I thought. He seemed so lost a few weeks ago. Maybe he still needs me as a friend. But isn't that what led me to getting back together with him a few years after graduation? Our on-again-off-again relationship had started seven years ago, as college sophomores. When we got back together after college, I thought we were "on" for good, but we simply weren't in the same place—geographically or in life.

I moved the cursor over and pushed "delete." "I'm giving him up for Lent," I resolved. It was Ash Wednesday, after all.

It hardly seems right to give up a person for Lent. At first, my lenten fast was a joke—a funny way to respond to my friend's sympathetic "How are you?" But pushing "delete" on that first e-mail made it a real fast. There would be no communication with my ex-boyfriend for the next forty days: no e-mail, no gchat, no text messages or phone calls, and especially no Facebook stalking. In today's world, it takes discipline to stay disconnected.

This fast was about more than discipline. My Lent was about embracing an uncertain future while not dwelling in the past. There were lonely nights at home and times when I just wanted to talk to somebody. Going out dancing with friends also made me depressed about the prospects of being single. "Is this it?" I asked a friend while we watched people throw themselves all over each other. Then, I'd go to Mass and the homily about love would hit too close to home.

In more positive moments, I'd realize that my mom answered the phone late into the night and let me be angry and crabby. My friends took me out dancing, had dinner with me, and offered their support and advice.

"Take some time to figure out who you are and what you want," one friend suggested. "Sure," I nodded, thinking to myself, "I'm twenty-seven. Shouldn't I know that already?"

It was in prayer that I realized that I didn't have myself figured out—as if any of us ever reach that point in our lives. As I thanked God for all those who were there for me, I realized that I hadn't always been there for them. I had neglected friendships in front of me in favor of a long-distance relationship. I lived in the future instead of the present. I wasn't who I wanted to be, but as a single person I could change that.

I could be there for my family and friends as they were there for me. I could give of myself to the wider community. There was an outlet for all the love and energy I had been directing three states away. Someday, I hoped, I would find a relationship that allows me to share my love more fully.

Forty days later, my joke of a fast had led to new life. It had seemed selfish to make Lent about me, but focusing inward actually took me outward, and I resolved to be there for others and seek out service opportunities during the Easter season.

Was I over him? It's hard to say, but the temptations to reach out to him waned. On Easter I was more eager to eat meat, which I fast from every Lent, than to check his Facebook profile.

I still mourned the future I saw with him—marriage and kids—and feared a future single and alone. But I also learned that single life isn't without love.

**Spiritual Principle: Hope**

Nothing really prepares you for the end of a relationship, which thrusts you fully back into the single state, whether you saw it coming weeks in advance or you were left feeling like someone pulled the rug out from underneath you. Perhaps you initiated the breakup or you were the reason of your partner desired to separate. Most breakups resemble the stages of grief: disbelief, denial, confusion, anger, bargaining, depression, and finally acceptance. Faced with ambiguity, you try to make sense of the past while simultaneously look ahead to an uncertain future.

Mom always said there were more fish in the sea. But in that moment of stunned disbelief, common clichés provide little consolation for a broken heart. Ironically, the universal symbol for hope is an anchor. An anchor is what grounds a boat in rough waters. It provides weight, so that a vessel doesn't go drifting off aimlessly into the dark. The anchor is what keeps a boat at bay in safe waters or the confines of a harbor. When it is difficult to see beyond the pain of past mistakes and fear of the future, it is easy to drift into despair. Hope is what helps us stay grounded in faith, rooted in prayer, weighted by the support of family, and strengthened among a trusted circle of friends. With time, when the seas are calm, we will be ready to venture out again.

Moving forward is only possible if we have hope. Hope is more than neat and tidy optimism. Hope begins in the messiness, the emptiness, and the unrealized dream for the future that suddenly comes crashing to an end. As we wait for the dust to settle and anticipate a return to life as "normal," it becomes painfully obvious that things will never be quite the same. There is no going back. Hope begins by taking stock of what remains. What lays broken, what needs to be let go, what pieces can be picked up and somehow salvaged from this mess? Hope requires that we be attentive to the scars and stretch marks that are the indicators of change. How am I different because of this? Is there anything for which I am grateful? What is one thing I gained?

Hope means letting go of the past, holding onto what is good, and reimagining the future. Hope requires that I slowly begin to let go of the things I said (or didn't say), the mistakes I made, the resentments I've held onto, and the way things could have been. In moments of loss and seasons of despair, hope sends us diving deeper in search of the things that are most valuable in life. What remains when all else is stripped away? What in my life, what of my purpose, my identity, my mission, and my values in life still remain? Maybe there is nothing obvious at first glance. But perhaps there is a tiny seed of hope buried deep in the darkness. People who have hope believe in a bigger vision, even when they're not exactly sure how to get there. Can I imagine what life might look like going forward? Can I see myself experiencing the joy of friendship, reveling in this time of freedom, or pursuing my dreams with greater integrity than before?

Finally, hope is a divine virtue. Guided by God's help, we are confident that God will provide all that we need to find happiness and love again. Hope is at the heart of the Paschal Mystery. This pattern of life, death, and resurrection that we find in Jesus is the path for all who walk the Christian journey. We will live and die and rise again just as Jesus did. New life will eventually rise from the ashes. Rarely do we have an opportunity to completely start over, but we do have second chances to start again. Starting again means that we take all that we have learned about ourselves and begin anew.

Hope is a risk. Hope dares to face the future certain that new life will come. It may not look like what we expected, and chances are it will look much different than it did before. It is hope that gives us the courage to step into the unknown and know that God moves us forward in the face of uncertainty.

Whether we find ourselves in the midst of a breakup or trying to mend a broken marriage, all is not lost. Hope dares us to believe that there is *more*, even when it seems like there is nothing left to give—even when life leaves us feeling empty, lonely, grieving, hurt, or confused. It is in that deep and apparent emptiness that we find God. And there hope, possibility, and new life begin to emerge.

**Scripture to Remember**

The LORD is near to the brokenhearted,
and saves the crushed in spirit. (Psalm 34:18)

For surely I know the plans I have for you, says the Lord, plans for your welfare and not for harm, to give you a future with hope. (Jeremiah 29:11)

May the God of hope fill you with all joy and peace in believing, so that you may abound in hope by the power of the Holy Spirit. (Romans 15:13)

**For Reflection**

1. Do I consider my future as a single person a hopeful or frightening prospect? How do I maintain hope in the face of uncertainty?
2. Do I continue to hold onto anger, resentment, or past mistakes? What of my past do I need to let go?
3. What are the lessons from the past that I can carry forward? Is there anything for which I am grateful? What is one thing I gained?

**Try This ...**

- Take yourself out on a date! Go to the movies, eat out at your favorite restaurant, attend a sporting event, or visit a museum by yourself. Allow yourself to be fully absorbed in the experience and savor every moment.
- Make a list of the qualities you seek in a relationship. Ask yourself: Do I meet the criteria that I seek in a partner? How can I better embody the positive qualities that I seek in someone else (good communication, compassion, sense of humor)?
- Pick your favorite holiday (Halloween, Independence Day, St. Patrick's Day, New Year's Eve) and find creative ways to celebrate! Decorate your cube or office door at work. Plan a theme party and invite your friends. Save money for a special trip to mark the occasion (just once I want to spend New Year's Eve in Time's Square!)
- Take time to do the things you love! Travel, photography, cooking, softball. It does not have to be big or elaborate. If you love to read, make a weekly visit to a used book store or your local library.
- Attend, plan, or volunteer at your favorite charity event. If it is a cause that you care about, you will feel good about giving to a worthy organization, have a great time, and most likely meet other people who are passionate about the same thing.
- Make a list of all the reasons why you like being single. Are there things in your life that are easier or come more naturally to you because you are single? In what areas of your life do you have "more" because you are single? Are you more mature, more independent, more confident, more generous? Do you have more time and flexibility?

- Consider the types of intimacy described in chapter fourteen—physical intimacy, emotional intimacy, intellectual intimacy, recreational intimacy, and spiritual intimacy. Make a list of the ways you find intimacy in each of these areas. Is there an aspect of intimacy that seems to be lacking, and if so, how can this be fulfilled?
- Imagine your eightieth birthday party. Who will be there? Where will it be held? Imagine the pictures people will show and the stories that will be told. Your best friend is invited to give a toast. What will this person say? How will people remember and celebrate your life?
- Make a list of all the things you've dreamed of doing, but always considered too risky, too foolish, or yourself too old to try (sailing around the world, taking ballet lessons, writing a novel.) What do the items on your list tell you about yourself? Is there a way to incorporate some small part of these things into your life? (If you wrote down Olympic figure skating, is there a local ice rink where you can rent skates?)
- For dealing with grief after a breakup, death, or other loss: Ask yourself, what is one good thing that I can hold onto or celebrate from this relationship? How can I carry a positive memory and move forward with my life?
- Draw a picture detailing the person or event you want to let go. Allow yourself to come to terms with what actually happened. Create a ritual for releasing the memory: X out the picture with bold paint, burn it, bury it, cut it into small pieces. Give yourself permission to let go of any lingering anger and resentment.

# NOTES


**Introduction**

1. Portions of this essay first appeared on BustedHalo.com in July 2005.

**Chapter One**

1. Henry David Thoreau, *Walden* (New York: Time, 1962), p. 88.

**Chapter Two**

1. Thomas Merton, *New Seeds of Contemplation* (New York: New Directions, 1972), p. 99.

**Chapter Five**

1. Ronald Rolheiser, *The Holy Longing: The Search for a Christian Spirituality* (New York: Doubleday, 1999), p. 93.
2. John Cariani, *Almost, Maine* (New York: Dramatists Play Service, 2007).

**Chapter Six**

1. Thomas Merton, *The Seven Storey Mountain* (New York: Harcourt Brace & Company, 1948), p. 458.

**Chapter Seven**

1. Paul Tillich, *The Eternal Now* (New York: Charles Scribner's Sons, 1963), pp. 17–18.
2. Joan Chittister, *Called to Question: A Spiritual Memoir* (Lanham, Md.: Sheed & Ward, 2004), p. 65.
3. Daniel Ladinsky, *Love Poems from God: Twelve Sacred Voices from the East and West* (New York: Penguin, 2002), p. 109.
4. Henri J.M. Nouwen, *Clowning in Rome: Reflections on Solitude, Celibacy, Prayer, and Contemplation* (New York: Image, 2000), p. 19.

**Chapter Eight**

1. Luci Swindoll, *Wide My World, Narrow My Bed: Living and Loving the Single Life* (Portland, Ore.: Multnomah, 1982), p. 70.
2. Patricia Sellers, "Melinda Gates goes public," *Fortune Magazine*, January 7, 2008. http://money.cnn.com/2008/01/04/news/ newsmakers/gates.fortune/index.htm.

**Chapter Nine**

1. Gregory F.A. Pierce, *Spirituality at Work* (Chicago: Loyola, 2001), p. 107.
2. Robert Wicks, *Everyday Spirituality: A Practical Guide to Spiritual Growth* (Notre Dame, Ind.: Sorin, 2000), pp. 46–47.

**Chapter Ten**

1. Khalil Gibran, *The Prophet* (New York: Knopf, 1973), pp. 58–59.
2. Richard Rohr, *From Wild Man to Wise Man: Reflections on Male Spirituality* (Cincinnati: St. Anthony Messenger Press, 2005), p. 17.
3. Aelred of Rievaulx, *Spiritual Friendship* (Collegeville, Minn.: Cistercian, 2005), pp. 92–93.

**Chapter Eleven**

1. Eileen E. O'Brien, "The Single Journey as Vocation," in *Single Women: Affirming Our Spiritual Journeys,* Mary O'Brien and Clare Christie, eds. (South Hadley, Mass.: Bergin & Garvey, 1993), p. 93.
2. Austin Flannery, ed. *Vatican Council II: The Basic Sixteen Documents* (Northport, N.Y.: Costello, 1996), p. 62.
3. Francine Cardman, "Singleness and Spirituality," *Spirituality Today* 35/4 (1983), pp. 304–318.
4. Tim Matovina, "Building Multicultural Parishes Requires More Than Sensitivity" *National Catholic Reporter.* July 27, 2001. http://natcath.org/NCR_Online/archives2/2001c/072701/072701r.htm.

**Chapter Twelve**

1. Pope John Paul II, *"Eucharistic Celebration: Homily of His Holiness John Paul II"* Apostolic Journey to the United States of America, Oriole Park at Camden Yards, Baltimore, Maryland. October 8, 1995.

**Chapter Thirteen**

1. Teresa of Avila, *The Interior Castle,* Kieran Kavanaugh and Otilio Rodriguez, trans. (New York: Paulist, 1979), p. 70.

**Chapter Fourteen**

1. Fran Ferder and John Heagle, *Tender Fires: The Spiritual Promise of Sexuality* (New York: Crossroad, 2001), p. 103.

# BIBLIOGRAPHY


Cardman, Francine. "Singleness and Spirituality," *Spirituality Today* 35/4, 1983.

Chapman, Gary. *The Five Love Languages for Singles.* Chicago: Northfield, 2004.

Hsu, Albert, Y. *Single at the Crossroads: A Fresh Perspective on Christian Singleness.* Westmont, Ill.: Intervarsity, 1997.

Jackowski, Karol. *10 Fun Things to Do Before You Die.* New York: Hyperion, 2000.

Kidder, Annemarie S. *Women, Celibacy, and the Church: Toward a Theology of the Single Life.* New York: Crossroad, 2003.

Martin, James. *My Life with the Saints.* Chicago: Loyola, 2006.

——. *Becoming Who You Are: Insights on the True Self from Thomas Merton and Other Saints.* Mahwah, N.J.: Hidden Spring, 2006.

Thomas Merton, *New Seeds of Contemplation.* New York: New Directions, 1972.

——. *Thoughts in Solitude.* New York: Farrar, Straus and Giroux, 1958.

Muto, Susan Annette. *Celebrating the Single Life: A Spirituality for Single Persons in Today's World.* New York: Crossroad, 1989.

Norris, Kathleen. *The Cloister Walk.* New York: Riverhead Trade, 1997.

Nouwen, Henri. *Clowning in Rome: Reflections on Solitude, Celibacy, Prayer and Contemplation* Garden City, N.Y.: Image, 2000.

——.*Out of Solitude: Three Meditations on the Christian Life.* Notre Dame, Ind.: Ave Maria, 2004.

O'Brien, Mary and Clare Christie, eds. *Single Women: Affirming Our Spiritual Journeys* Westport, Conn.: Bergin & Garvey, 1993.

Sheridan, Jean. *The Unwilling Celibates: A Spirituality for Single Adults.* New London, Conn.: Twenty-Third, 2000.

Swindoll, Luci. *Wide My World, Narrow My Bed: Living and Loving the Single Life.* Sisters, Oreg.: Multnomah, 1982.

Tillich, Paul. *The Eternal Now.* New York: Scribner, 1963.

Whitehead, Evelyn Eaton and James D. Whitehead, *A Sense of Sexuality: Christian Love and Intimacy.* New York: Doubleday, 1989.

# ABOUT THE CONTRIBUTORS

**Clarissa V. Aljentera** combines her passion for writing, ministry, and communication as a campus minister for the Sheil Catholic Center at Northwestern University's Chicago campus. She also writes and speaks about Facebook, ministry, and young adults. Before entering ministry, Clarissa worked as a newspaper journalist. Originally from California, she enjoys hanging out by the ocean.

**Julia Benson** embraces her one single life in the city of Chicago where she teaches science to seventh and eighth graders and pursues interests related to music, knitting, and community involvement. Julia grew up in Iowa and completed her undergraduate degree at Duke University. She is thankful for this opportunity to reflect on the spirituality of singleness and continues to listen for the still small voice of God's call.

**Sarah Coles** was born and raised in New Orleans and is the product of many years of Catholic education. She received a bachelor of science in elementary education from Spring Hill College and a master of divinity degree from Loyola University, Chicago. Sarah is currently the director of religious education at a Chicago parish and is preparing to return to New Orleans to continue her work in ministry with youth and young adults.

**Mary O'Brien Danek** was raised in River Forest, Illinois, and attended St. Luke Grade School, Trinity High School, and Dominican University. She holds a bachelor's degree in English, a master's degree in education and elementary and secondary teacher certification. Mary and her husband, Robert, live in Geneva, Illinois, where she enjoys life as a stay-at-home mom for twin daughters, Maeve and Bernadette, seven, and son, Stephen, five.

**Lisa Furney** is a certified American Sign Language interpreter, obtaining her interpreting degree from Iowa Western Community College and her bachelor's degree from Central College. She has been an active member in the Methodist church all her life. She is interested in not only singles ministry, but for *all* people to make connections in small groups. She was born, raised, and still lives in Iowa.

**Christine Harrell** teaches at Head Start in inner-city Chicago. She earned a bachelor of science in early childhood education from De Paul University and a master's in education at Christian Brothers University. She is a member of Teachers for Social Justice and active in S.E.I.U. Healthcare Illinois. Christine also studies flamenco dance at Clinard Dance Theater, attends book club meetings, and participates in ReCiL, a Catholic young adult group in Chicago.

**Mike Hays** is a campus minister at St. Joseph University Parish, which serves the State University of New York at Buffalo. Mike authored the book *Googling God* (Paulist 2007), blogs on marriage, prayer, and spiritual experience at GooglingGod.com, and founded the website BustedHalo.com. He is married to Marion, and they live in Amherst, New York, with their dog, Haze.

**Katie Kustusch** is a Missionary of Compassion with Heart's Home International in Bangkok, Thailand. She previously worked in communications at the Sheil Catholic Center at Northwestern University. She also served as the project manager for the *One Body One Spirit Project*, a nonprofit organization dedicated to building relationships within the global Catholic community. Katie is a fourth-generation Chicago native and holds a bachelor's degree in German from North Central College.

**Allison Leigh** is a campus minister at the University of Dayton in Dayton, Ohio. She earned a master's in pastoral ministry from the University of Dayton and a bachelor of fine arts from Xavier University. When not planning retreats, she can be found doing freelance graphic design work, running, and riding her bike.

**Bekah Stolhandske McNeel** grew up in Texas. She studied at the Master's College and received her master's in science from the London School of Economics before responding to God's call to ministry. Bekah currently works as a counselor and develops ministry resources for Reformed University Fellowship. She recently married and lives in San Antonio with her husband, Lewis.

**Mark Mossa, S.J.,** a Jesuit priest, studies and teaches theology at Fordham University in New York City. In addition to teaching, he is actively involved in campus and other young adult ministries. He wrote *Already There: Letting God Find You* and *St. Ignatius Loyola: The Spiritual Writings*, annotated and explained. He is a frequent speaker on topics in American Catholicism, popular culture, young adult ministry, and spirituality.

**Abby Nall** is a speech-language pathologist who received a master's in science from Rush University in 2009. Abby is a member and past president of the Ravenswood Catholic Young Adult Group, a multi-parish partnership in Chicago which organizes spiritual, service, and social activities. After years of enjoying a rich and meaningful single life, Abby married Mike in May 2011.

**Christina Maria Paschyn,** an international multimedia journalist, holds a bachelor's and a master's degree in broadcast journalism from Northwestern University's Medill School of Journalism. Most recently, Christina traveled to Israel on a Rotary International

Ambassadorial scholarship and received a master's degree in Middle East studies from Ben-Gurion University.

**Joanne Singleton,** originally from Scotland, holds a bachelor of arts in sports science from University of Chester, and a master's in social work from University of Nebraska. She is a licensed clinical social worker working with children receiving liver and intestinal transplants at Children's Memorial Hospital in Chicago. An avid runner, she has completed ten marathons and holds a personal record of 3 hours 29 minutes.

**Megan Sweas,** a journalist from Chicago, currently serves as associate editor for *U.S. Catholic* magazine, where she covers social justice issues and young adults, among other topics. After graduating from the Medill School of Journalism at Northwestern University, she completed a year of service through Amate House, a full-time Catholic volunteer program for young adults.

**Maggi Van Dorn** began studying theology at Santa Clara University, where she developed an Ignatian appetite for "seeing God in all things," the effects of which have led to regular blogging at maggivandorn.blogspot.com. She is now a student at Harvard Divinity School, and in a committed relationship to spirituality and the arts.

## About the Author

Beth M. Knobbe lives an intentional single life. She earned a master of divinity degree from Catholic Theological Union in Chicago and serves as a campus minister at the Sheil Catholic Center at Northwestern University. She is a regular speaker on young adult spirituality and the author of *Finding My Voice: A Young Woman's Perspective* (St. Anthony Messenger Press, 2009).